the heart of worship files

COMPILED BY

matt REDMAN

Regal

From Gospel Light
Ventura, California, U.S.A.

Regal

PUBLISHED BY REGAL BOOKS
FROM GOSPEL LIGHT
VENTURA, CALIFORNIA, U.S.A.
PRINTED IN THE U.S.A.

Regal Books is a ministry of Gospel Light, an evangelical
Christian publisher dedicated to serving the local church. We
believe God's vision for Gospel Light is to provide church leaders
with biblical, user-friendly materials that will help them evange-
lize, disciple and minister to children, youth and families.

It is our prayer that this Regal book will help you discover
biblical truth for your own life and help you meet the
needs of others. May God richly bless you.

*For a free catalog of resources from Regal Books/Gospel Light,
please call your Christian supplier or contact us at* 1-800-4-GOSPEL
or www.regalbooks.com.

Rights for publishing this book in other languages are contracted
by Gospel Light Worldwide, the international nonprofit
ministry of Gospel Light. Gospel Light Worldwide also provides
publishing and technical assistance to international publishers
dedicated to producing Sunday School and Vacation Bible
School curricula and books in the languages of the world. For
additional information, visit www.gospellightworldwide.org;
write to Gospel Light Worldwide, P.O. Box 3875, Ventura, CA
93006; or send an e-mail to info@gospellightworldwide.org.

This edition issued by special arrangement with Kingsway Publications, Lottbridge Drove, Eastbourne, East Sussex, England, BN23 6NT.

Library of Congress Cataloging-in-Publication Data
The heart of worship files / [compiled by] Matt Redman.
     p. cm.
  ISBN 0-8307-3261-6
1.   Public worship. I. Redman, Matt.
  BV15 .H38 2003
  264—dc21   2002155751

1 2 3 4 5 6 7 8 9 10 / 09 08 07 06 05 04 03

CONTENTS

INTRODUCTION

MATT REDMAN

The Church today is full of new songs and sounds. Look around and you'll find so many creative approaches to leading worship—signs of love and life from an adoring Bride. We are a singing Church. We journey on for the Kingdom come, treading with reverence and shouting for joy. It's an exciting time to be involved in leading God's people in worship through music.

Into this environment was born *heartofworship.com*—as an online resource to encourage, challenge and inspire lead worshippers along the way. *The Heart of Worship Files* is a collection of highlights from the website.

We have compiled the readings in this book, keeping in mind that there are various, different sides to leading worship. The compilation provides practical advice for the pastoral aspects of worship leading, creative advice for the musical side of things and perceptive insights into the theology of worship. It also delves into our heritage for some inspiration from musical worshippers of the past. Each reading fits into one of five categories: Practical Worship Leading, Creative Insight, Songwriting, Theology of Worship and Searching the Psalms. Each category is represented by an icon that you'll see in the contents and at the top of the corresponding pages of the book. You'll also find a recurring section called The One Thing, which contains responses from experienced lead worshippers when asked, "What is the one thing most on your heart for those involved in leading worship these days?"

Some of the material in this book is a fairly light-hearted read and easy to get to grips with. Other sections might require a little more serious study. We hope this mixture will both inspire and instruct you in your walk of worship.

Most of all, we pray that these highlights from *heartof worship.com* will sharpen you in your quest to know Jesus and make Him known to others.

creative insight

REVELATION AND RESPONSE

MATT REDMAN

Recently I've been considering worship through the windows of revelation and response. What kind of revelation do the songs we use bring to the people who sing them? Do they paint a big picture of God? Is there enough of His grace and splendor in our worship meetings to awaken even tired, discouraged hearts? And are we responding in a way that fits the revelation received? Worship is always a response to a revelation.

As I look at these two aspects of worship, I see I've paid more attention to one of them than the other. I often find myself approaching congregational worship much more mindful of the response element than of the revelation side of things. And I wonder if that isn't the case for many other lead worshippers, too.

In some church services, it's obvious that the worship leader is consumed, above all else, with getting a response from the people. Not much is implied about the integrity and heart of the offerings. Instead comes a barrage of forceful encouragements to shout, clap, dance or anything else you can think of. Instead of focusing on bringing a true and meaningful overflow of the heart, leaders have settled for some sort of spiritual disco competition with a prize for the wildest participant. Yes, it's easy to point the finger. But am I so very different when I lead worship? What's going on inside my head when I lead?

Haven't I led meetings during which my mind gets the clap-o-meter out at the end of every celebration song to check if we're on course? After all, if people clap at the end of each up-tempo song, that means we're in for a good night, doesn't it? Don't I sometimes find myself subconsciously scanning the congregational horizon for any sign of life? Some outstretched hands, perhaps—that definitely means its working! And as we move into intimate reverence, don't I sometimes squint through my half-closed eyes to see what other responses are happening, hoping to see at least one person on their knees or in tears?

I'm exaggerating to make a point, but I hope the point is clear: Too often when I lead worship I'm driven to get a good response out of the people. I want to see results.

Now, all of these things—dancing, lifting up holy hands, clapping and kneeling—are potentially good things. But rather than being so desperate to see these things happen (or God forbid, even trying to make them happen), I should be far more interested in what lies behind these responses (or the lack of them). It's a subtle distinction but an important one for the mind-set of any lead worshipper.

> LET'S BRING SONGS SO FULL OF OUR GLORIOUS JESUS THAT THEY IGNITE A HEART-FILLED RESPONSE IN THOSE WHO SING THEM.

And that takes us right back to revelation. Before we become consumed with how people are responding, it's good to be mindful of what they're responding to. As worship leaders and songwriters, we need to pay more attention to the reasons for God's worth in our writing and leading. What aspects of His wonder and splendor are we presenting for people to get their hearts into? How are we reminding hearts, minds and souls of the merciful acts that God has done for them and the amazing grace that He has won for them?

Of course, this isn't just our responsibility—everyone involved in the service plays a part. But we must take our role seriously. Instead of trying to work people up (however subtly) to some sort of response, let's take a different approach. Let's bring songs so full of our glorious Jesus that they ignite a fresh fire and a heart-filled response from those who sing them.

William Temple once wrote:

> To worship is to quicken the conscience by the
>   holiness of God,
> To feed the mind with the truth of God,
> To purge the imagination by the beauty of God,
> To open the heart to the love of God,
> To devote the will to the purpose of God.[1]

Notice how much Temple's definition of worship is centered around revelation. Here's a man who knew that to get people caught up in the holiness, truth and beauty of God results in the devotion of their wills to the purpose of God. Our whole lives need to be poured out in worship. And in the end, that is the ultimate response of anyone who has truly recognized the all-consuming revelation of God.

If, in the power of the Holy Spirit, we can help usher people into a fresh revelation of Jesus during our worship times, the response will take care of itself. We will not be able to stand in the way of a room of passionate, dancing, shouting, bowing, adoring lovers of God.

the one thing...

GRAHAM KENDRICK

Pursue the biggest vision of Christ you can. My reference Bible records 101 different names and titles by which Jesus is revealed in the Bible, each one a key to knowing more of who we are worshipping and why. Worship is a response and will grow or shrink in direct proportion to our view of Him. We love to worship Christ as Savior and Friend, but how often do we worship Him as Judge or Author of Life or Desired of All Nations? Seek out; use; and if you are able, write truth-saturated songs that stretch the minds and hearts of the worshipping Church to grasp as much as we can of His incredible glories and cosmic purposes.

REFLECTIONS ON PSALM 8

(PART 1)

LOUIE GIGLIO

Little Leaders

O LORD, our Lord, how majestic is your name in all the earth.

PSALM 8:1

When worship is the subject, little leaders are what we need. I don't necessarily mean small in stature but small in terms of self, for there is no other enemy of true worship besides self.

As a result of the Fall, we all have a deadly preoccupation with ourselves. We are self-aware, self-focused, self-conscious, self-made, self-protecting, self-promoting, self-centered and selfish. Conversion to Christ is nothing less than getting over ourselves. That's why there is more than a subtle change that happens at the foot of the Cross. A death takes place there. Christianity is not about self-help but rather self-death. New life begins when we each abandon "me" and fall on the mercy of a God who loves us in spite of ourselves and a Christ who gave Himself in our place. In that moment, we embrace freedom from the perpetual doom of the flesh and take up the cause of living solely for the One who freed us. Such is the way of the Savior, who calls any who would be a recipient of new life to "*deny yourself*, take up your cross daily, and follow me" (see Matt. 16:24).

Yet from my experience, self does not go quietly. Instead, it stubbornly rears its head and demands its way, looking for any opportunity to stand in the limelight and receive the glory. If left unchecked, self will stand in the light of God and somehow try to take credit for it.

Recently, I was stunned by a photograph in *USA Today* of what astronomers say is the perfect spiral galaxy. Taken with the help of a new telescope on the Big Island of Hawaii, the photo shows a breathtaking shot of a galaxy named NGC 628—slightly smaller than our Milky Way (it contains only a paltry 100 billion stars) and, get this, 30 million light-years away. Funny, the whole point of the accompanying article was *our* great achievement of taking such a great photograph with *our* two-week-old telescope. Aren't *we* great? Hmmm. Seems like all the wrong pronouns! Granted, we have done well to photograph anything 30 million light-years away, but let's get the point straight: God's hand put every one of those stars in place. An appropriate caption for this photo would have been, "Can you believe God made this stuff with His own hands?"

The psalmist writes:

When I consider your heavens, the work of your fingers, the moon and the stars, which you have set in place, what is man that you are mindful of him, the son of man that you care for him? (Ps. 8:3-4).

Notice all the pronouns. *Your* heavens. *Your* fingers. *You* set in place. Get it? God is far from small. In fact, it's safe to say our self-limitation has never fully allowed us to think of Him as He is. Given His incomprehensible immensity, the fact that He is mindful of us at all is amazing!

So if you want a quick glimpse into how small you are as a leader, take note of which pronouns consume you: "His," "He" and "Yours"; or "I," "me" and "mine." Little leaders use "He" a lot. The big ones use "me."

A stage is a dangerous place to be, because a stage, by definition, is a raised platform. Stages are built so that little people can be seen more easily by larger audiences. The lights are bright. The sound is big. Yet if we are not careful, those of us who lead worship can allow the stage to succeed, making more of us than we really are.

It's not that we are nobodies. We're created a little lower than angels and are crowned with glory and honor—made in His image (see Ps. 8:5). We get to rule over all He has made. But we've only to look up to be resized in an instant.

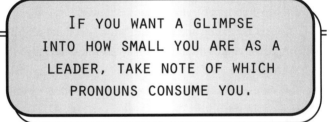

IF YOU WANT A GLIMPSE INTO HOW SMALL YOU ARE AS A LEADER, TAKE NOTE OF WHICH PRONOUNS CONSUME YOU.

Rather than absorb the light that shines on leaders, we must continually reflect it back to God. One night my wife, Shelley, and I were flying home to Waco from Houston in a small twin-engine plane. Every time I looked out the window, I saw a massive searchlight moving rapidly across the ground below. At first I thought a police helicopter was tracking some criminals, but after an hour the light was still there. Finally I spoke up, wondering aloud what could be going on. The pilot, ever so confident, informed me that the moon (which was full at the time and pretty much right there, if I'd only looked up) was shining on the plane, reflecting a huge circle of light onto the ground.

I felt like an idiot! Embarrassed and a little humiliated, I went back to minding my own business. Then it hit me! Eager to get even, I remarked that actually the moon was not shining on the plane. Rather, the sun was shining on the moon (hah!), and the light of the sun was reflecting off the moon onto the plane. Thus the sunlight was making the huge searchlight on the ground. Brilliant!

Well, as far as lead worshippers go, we need more little moons. Shine a light on them if you will, but you'll only see a greater reflection of His glory in all those around them.

"O LORD, our Lord, how majestic is your name in all the earth!" (Ps. 8:1).

the one thing...

(MIKE PILAVACHI)

Here are the questions that have challenged me recently:
How many songs do we sing that are just about God and
do not bring us into the story? How often is God not only
the object but also the center of our worship? I am sure we
need to sing more songs that praise Him for who He is,
irrespective of what He has done for us. The worship of
heaven, as we see in Revelation 4 and 5, is amazing in its
color, sound and participants. The 4 living creatures and
the 24 elders seem to be having a great time as they take it
in turns to sing their songs and fall down. A few million
angels and then every creature join them. Great sight.
Great noise. But incomplete. The centerpiece comes as
the grand finale: the One who sits on the throne and the
Lamb. The rest are incidental: the audience, the support-
ing cast.

How God-centered is my worship? Maybe I need to
tell Him a little less about me—what I feel and what I am
going to do—and focus a little more on Him.

WE BECOME LIKE WHAT
WE WORSHIP

(D O N   W I L L I A M S)

Worship money, become a greedy person. Worship sex, become a lustful person. Worship power, become a corrupt person. Worship Jesus, become a Christlike person. We become like what we worship. But what does it mean to worship?

The verb "worship" in Hebrew means to surrender, to fall down in submission—the way we would humble ourselves before a mighty king (see Ps. 95:6). Paul says that worship is the offering of our bodies as a sacrifice (see Rom. 12:1). This worship goes on in all of our lives. While we may fail to understand it, worship is the spiritual part of our surrender, submission and attachment to many things. The worship of money or sex or power or people results in addictive and compulsive behaviors. The staggering truth is that we all are lured into worshipping something or someone other than the living God. This is idolatry—pure and simple. It steals our humanity and addicts us. So if we are really to be free from idolatry, we must understand addiction.

Addiction happens when we attach our desire to alcohol or street drugs or sex or gambling or money or a person who controls us or whatever else. As that attachment grows, it consumes us. Little by little, we become captive to the very thing that gives us pleasure and meaning. Dr. Gerald May says, "We are all addicts in every sense of the word."[1] If this is true, then we also are idolaters in every sense of the word. You say, "Not me, Don." But remember, denial is the first symptom of addiction.

Psychologist John Bradshaw says that most of us come from dysfunctional families—families that don't work in an open, healthy way. Perhaps we were often abused as children, either sexually, physically or verbally. As a result, we live with a lot of repressed pain. Bradshaw calls this the hole in the soul. We will stuff anything into it in order to fill it up. It is a magnet for addictions. And it only grows larger—nothing satisfies.[2]

If idolatry is the issue and addiction the result, how can we understand it? The three Cs provide a handle. Addiction starts with *craving*; this leads to *control loss*; and the result is *continuing use*. Let's say we build a dependency on nicotine. When we need a fix to relax or lift our mood, the craving sets in. The more we use, the more we want (and need). We are now out of control, on our way to chain-smoking. Once addicted, we are in the continual-use pattern. When this becomes an obsession, it becomes an idol.

> **WHATEVER THE OBJECTS OF OUR ADDICTIONS ARE, THEY BECOME IDOLS IN OUR LIVES.**

What then is the root of addiction? It is spiritual; it is idolatry. Whatever the objects of our addictions are, they become idols in our lives. We become preoccupied with them, crave them and serve them. As we have seen, worshipping them is the spiritual side of addiction. The Bible teaches that we not only dishonor God with our idols, but we also lose our true humanity:

> But their idols are silver and gold, made by the hands of men. Those who make them will be like them, and so will all who trust in them (Ps. 115:4,8).

Jeremiah 2:5 says, "They followed worthless idols and became worthless themselves."

In *Bringing the Church to the World*, Tom Wright analyzes idolatry. First, idols are all a perversion of the good. For example, sex is good, under God's design and plan. As an idol, it is degraded, and it enslaves us. Second, idols enhance us. When we worship them, we feel 10 feet tall. Third, idols demand sacrifice. Every addict knows what he or she has sacrificed to the idol of alcohol or drugs—time, energy, money, integrity and even other people. Fourth, we create an ideology to justify our idols. Sexual obsession becomes the sexual revolution—the conquest of damaging, Victorian repression. Fifth, idols enslave us. They demand our lives. No wonder Paul teaches that behind the dumb idols lurk demons (see 1 Cor. 10:19-20). They want to hold us in the kingdom of darkness.[3]

The Bible carries on a continual battle with idolatry. The first commandment is "You shall have no other gods before me" (Exod. 20:3). The second is "You shall not make for yourself an idol" (Exod. 20:4). God alone is worthy of our worship. In this, He gives us back our true selves.

If we become what we worship, then the road out of idolatry is to renounce our idols and turn to the living God. This begins with a personal, public surrender. In psychological language, we must detach. This can only come by God's gracious intervention. Moral conviction will not do it. Only brokenness at the center of our being will do it. Only cutting through our shame and guilt will do it.

Paul writes in Romans 12:1:

> Therefore, I urge you, brothers, in view of God's mercy, to offer your bodies as living sacrifices, holy and pleasing to God—this is your spiritual act of worship.

By this mercy, then, we come to worship. We bring the sacrifice of our bodies, and they are acceptable to God through the perfect, sinless body of His Son.

Next we ask the Spirit of God to fill the hole in the soul with Himself. We begin to worship God alone—to love Him with all our heart, mind, soul and strength. This worship will cause us to be Christlike. Rather than our being conformed to this world and our idolatrous addictions, He will conform us to Himself (see Rom. 12:2). Worship drugs, become a depressed or burned-out person. Worship work, become a restless, frantic person. Worship people, become a selfish, dependent person. Worship Jesus, become a Christlike person.

We become like what we worship. We are either like the idols or like the living God. We must make our choice. Paul tells the Thessalonians:

> You turned to God from idols to serve the living and true God, and to wait for his Son from heaven, whom he raised from the dead—Jesus, who rescues us from the coming wrath (1 Thess. 1:9-10).

There really is no other option.

the one thing...

SALLY MORGANTHALER

As a young worship leader, I focused on creating worship experiences, on making sure people felt like they'd met God before they left. As a worship planner, I still ask myself the question, *How are people going to encounter God in this time of worship?* But increasingly, I'm focusing on the God of our experience, not the experience itself. The reason for this is that it's entirely possible to feel close to God without really focusing on who He is. It's entirely possible to work ourselves into a worship euphoria without distinguishing between god generic and God incarnate. And in this age of spiritual pluralism, that difference is pivotal.

Worship leaders: Do we lead people into the throne room of a generic god, or do we draw them into the presence of the One, revealed and made eternally accessible to us in Jesus Christ? Let's introduce a waiting world to the Father. But may it only be through the Son and by the power of the Holy Spirit. Worship leading is more than crafting awesome God experiences. It is introducing people to the awesome God of the experience—Creator, Redeemer and Sustainer.

THOUGHTS ON SONGWRITING

(PART 1)

Making Melody

There are perhaps two main types of melody writers—those who stumble across tunes (like me) and those who know about music theory and therefore might take a more thought-out approach. Whichever type you are, make sure you write from your heart.

The best congregational melodies work *in* worship because they began *as* worship. Write songs that are easy to learn and hard to forget. Melodies that can be memorized straight away yet also have a catchy, lingering tune that stays in your head long after the moment.

One other thing—in most types of music, the chords are just as important as the melody line itself. It's always good to run the melody line through several different chord progressions, just to see what happens. You may come across a beautiful match between tune and chord, which you weren't planning for originally.

Matt Redman

Be yourself. Let the melody flow naturally from your personality. Don't evaluate too quickly. You can't be self-conscious at this stage—you must let yourself feel. Mechanical melodies don't move people—human ones do. I find I need some space, time and privacy at this point; I can't be thinking about someone's listening at this stage; I just have to let go—which usually means singing some things that sound . . . well, goofy! Once the basic melody is there, then step back and evaluate: Is it memorable? Is there a strong motif holding each section of the song together?

Finally, make sure your high point melodically is your high point lyrically. It doesn't really help the song if your highest and climatic note comes on the word "and"!

Brian Doerksen

Of course, everyone has a different approach to this. I once heard Willie Nelson (an American folk legend!) say that melodies are all around us in the air, that we just have to grab them. I kind of like that. It's a bit abstract, but it's a good picture. When grabbing for one of them, keep your congregation in mind. Remember that most people are musically illiterate. Keep the rhythm of the lyrics simple. Try to create space within the song. While you should keep in mind the vocal ranges for both men and women, it's sometimes appropriate to place melodies on the edge of these ranges to cause people to really sing out.

Chris Tomlin

First, listen to many styles of music. Having a wide range of musical input increases your chances of good musical output. Second, try to develop melody without your instrument. This can help you avoid getting stuck in a playing rut where one chord always naturally progresses to another. Third, try to write melody and lyrics together sometimes—this can really help form the direction and tone of the song.

Martyn Layzell

Match the language of the words with that of the music so that the melody brings to life the text and the text enhances the music.

There are limitless possibilities in the composition of melody. A great deal can be communicated with very little. The intervals of the notes within a melody—whether based on the modal system or the major and minor scales, or perhaps influenced by Indian or Oriental scales—create a language and mood of impression.

> OUR DUTY AND OUR JOY IS TO PUT NEW MELODIES AND INSPIRING HEAVENLY MUSIC ONTO THE LIPS AND INTO THE HEARTS OF GOD'S CHILDREN.

As composers and writers of melody in the sphere of sacred music, we must make time to quietly listen to the language that speaks to our hearts and minds—the still small voice of our great and wonderful God of love, our inspirational Creator. In humility of heart and purpose may we then bring something of heaven down to Earth in our music. Our duty and our joy is to put new melodies and inspiring heavenly music onto the lips and into the hearts of God's children.

Dave Clifton

Work with hooks—in other words, little melodies that hook themselves in your head. We all know songs that have good hooks—they're the ones we remember and want to sing over and over. You only need one or two hooks in a song, and as long as the rest of the melody is good, it will sing really well. Also make sure the melody is simple enough to learn yet interesting enough for people to want to sing time and again.

Kathryn Scott

It's very hard to put into words the process of writing a melody. Personally, I need to record all of my ideas and then give them time to form. I have a minidisc packed full of song ideas. It takes me weeks, even months, to fully form these tunes. The temptation is to rush it and assume a tune is finished, but melodies can almost always be improved.

The key thing in evaluating melodies is to ask yourself, *Is it singable?* Is it a tune you enjoy singing and you find that it's catchy, even when you sing it away from your instrument? If so, then you're on to something! This issue of singability is crucial. You can have the most inspired, poetic lyrics, drenched in biblical truth; but if the tune is dull or awkward to sing, it may never work as a congregational worship song.

Tim Hughes

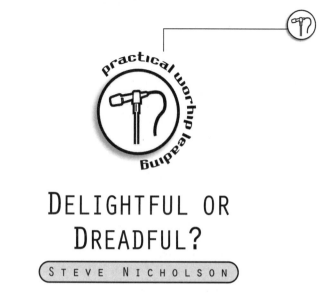

practical worship leading

DELIGHTFUL OR DREADFUL?

(STEVE NICHOLSON)

As a pastor, I've been working with worship leaders for over 25 years. Generally it's been a positive experience. My current worship pastor and I have been working together for 12 years and we're looking forward to many more. Yet there have been some times when my interactions with worship leaders have left me groaning inside. So what's the difference? What makes some such a delight and others such a sorrow?

You might expect me to focus on the intricacies of pastor-worship leader relationships. But this time I'd like to assume that there are no problems there and focus on other qualities instead—three to delight in and three to dread.

QUALITIES TO DELIGHT IN

1. A Love for Worshipping Jesus That Is Readily Seen

There's nothing quite so powerful as simply worshipping behind the leadership of someone who really loves worshipping Jesus and somehow has the ability to let that be seen by the congregation. It doesn't have to be over the top; it just has to be genuine and expressed somehow. Sometimes it's a matter of how the songs are sung. Sometimes it's a matter of how the songs are chosen. Not everyone who genuinely loves worship is able to let others see it from the stage and then participate in it. But when that does happen, even the simplest songs can take us to heaven.

2. A Commitment to Be a Functioning Disciple and Church Member Who Sometimes Happens to Lead Worship

Worship leaders need to be genuinely connected to their churches. This can be evidenced by things like staying and listening to the sermons rather than hiding backstage when not leading worship, joining in the prayer times, building relationships with those who are not musicians, being open about their need to keep learning and growing

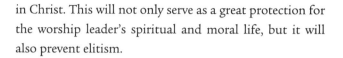

in Christ. This will not only serve as a great protection for the worship leader's spiritual and moral life, but it will also prevent elitism.

3. A Healthy Balance Between Hanging On to the Tried-and-True Ways and Songs of Worship from the Past, and a Continual Development of Fresh Ways of Worshipping God

If their worship is not to become routine and stagnant, congregations need a continual (but not too steep) growth curve—fresh ways of worshipping God, including new songs and the like. At the same time, we need to stay connected to the best of the past—both the more recent past and the past of previous generations. This is going to require a lot of study, research and work on the part of the worship leader. But over the long haul, it will help produce a healthier congregation of worshippers.

QUALITIES TO DREAD

1. The Performance Mentality

It's all too easy for worship leaders to become rock-and-roll stars who perform songs with Christian lyrics. The focus shifts onto the music, and we end up with a show that lacks any thought for whether it is helping the folks in the back row get connected with God in worship. When this performance mentality starts to take hold, it's usually seen in a kind of elitism: acting like a professional band

> THE PERFORMANCE MENTALITY WILL INFECT THE CHURCH WITH ATTITUDES LIKELY TO KILL GENUINE WORSHIP OF JESUS.

that hides out backstage or elsewhere when not leading worship (i.e., the music is the only time and way that the worship leader is involved with the church or congregation), hangs out only with musicians and does things because they showcase talents rather than because they help ordinary people worship. Or even more subtle, they do songs that are difficult to sing by untrained musicians. All these things will ultimately infect the Church with attitudes likely to kill genuine worship of Jesus.

2. The Lone Ranger Mentality

I've seen some worship leaders—leaders who genuinely love

worshipping Jesus—leave the congregation way behind as they go off into the heights of their own personal worship and creativity. They are having a good worship experience, it seems, but only a few others can manage to join with them. This can happen when songs are too complex to sing or when the worship leader goes off into long impromptu worship, leaving the congregation wondering what they are supposed to sing or do next. I've seen some worship leaders drift off into the wild blue yonder with their eyes shut for 30 to 40 minutes, not once noticing that they had lost 85 percent of the congregation, who were standing there watching in silence. It's important to remember that the job of the worship leader is to help a congregation of ordinary people (most of them not trained musicians) worship God in a meaningful and par-ticipatory way.

3. The Artsy Mentality

By this I mean the attitude that conveys it's more impor-tant for the worship leader to explore, develop and display his or her artistic and creative abilities than to help the people enter into worship. Sometimes this is done in the name of "This is to attract the artsy people who might come." But if the people who are already there and ready to worship God are excluded in the process, then nothing of lasting value is going to be accomplished. Perhaps there are good places for this exploration of artistic ability to take place, but a worship service is not one of them—unless one has a unique congregation of only musicians and artistic people.

All of these qualities, both positive and negative, are based on actual experiences I have had. The fact that you're reading this means you're already genuinely concerned with how to grow and be a good worship leader. But my hope is that this will encourage you to keep developing in the three delightful qualities listed here, while watching out for the three dreadful ones.

the one thing...

JOHN WILLISON

Short of loving Jesus Himself, the one thing I'd say is to love the Church, His Bride. Carry the Church in your heart—all the different kinds of people. Think about her during your day. Love her. Protect her. Honor her. Don't let anyone use her, abuse her or say anything bad about her. Make your decisions for the betterment of the Church—your songs, your list, your personnel and your training of others.

Only let people who truly love the Church serve the Church and lead the Church.

songwriting

REFRESHING HYMNS

MATT REDMAN

Have you ever been leading worship and not been able to find the right song for that moment? Maybe a song of lament was needed, but you didn't really know any. Or the pastor asked for a song responding to the holiness of God, but again you couldn't seem to find an appropriate one for that theme.

If you're anything like me, you'll have been in this kind of situation a few times. I'm realizing more and more that as worship leaders, we need to widen our song vocabulary—songs for every biblical theme and songs for every walk of life.

In light of this, I've been delving into a few old hymn books, and I'm seeing a depth and breadth of lyrical content that we cannot afford to ignore. As worship leaders, we have an amazing heritage: throughout the ages many of the saints have poured their hearts out to God through song. So many of these hymns and songs resound with our hearts even now. It's a faith-building thing, too, to realize that hundreds of years ago these writers were meeting with

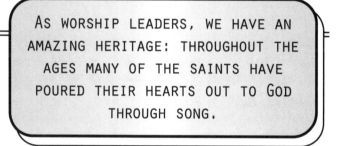

AS WORSHIP LEADERS, WE HAVE AN AMAZING HERITAGE: THROUGHOUT THE AGES MANY OF THE SAINTS HAVE POURED THEIR HEARTS OUT TO GOD THROUGH SONG.

and responding to the very same Jesus we encounter today. So many of these old hymn writers and their hymns have much to teach us about writing poetic, biblical songs, and I for one have decided I want to become their student. I'm hungry for everything I can get my hands on.

A friend of mine recently gave me a copy of an old Methodist hymnbook he found in his attic. The book is a collection of Methodist Protestant hymns, published in Baltimore, Maryland, in 1849. As soon as I opened the first page, I knew I was in for an education. I have never seen such a diverse collection of biblical themes in one book.

The first section goes through the attributes of God and includes His wisdom, holiness, justice, goodness, truth, faithfulness, Trinity, mercy, love, eternity, omnipresence and omnipotence. Pretty impressive. But that's only just the start. Next we discover a list of hymns on some of the relations of God (i.e., who He is to us): Maker, Preserver and Sovereign.

We then get into the works of God, which come in three sections: Creation, Providence and Redemption. In the third section there are hymns covering every imaginable angle of our redemption: love of the Father, character of Christ, promise of Christ, types of Christ, birth of Christ, life of Christ, death of Christ, resurrection of Christ, ascension of Christ, intercession of Christ, reign of Christ, second coming of Christ, offices of Christ and titles of Christ. Again, a pretty extensive list!

The next section has 12 pages of hymns that respond to and call on the Holy Spirit: songs on the promise of the Holy Spirit, the descent of the Holy Spirit, the operations of the Spirit, prayers for the Spirit and addresses to the Spirit.

Let me warn you: at this point we are not even one third of the way through the hymnbook! Next we get into songs about the Church—songs for times of revival in the

Church and songs for times of declension (i.e., when things aren't going too great!).

The themes just keep on coming: salvation, repentance, faith, justification, our adoption, hope, humility, joy, love, wisdom, the mind of Christ, triumph in death, glory in the resurrection, immortality in heaven and the worship of God for His judgments.

Then we get down to the Private Devotion section: songs to sing before you go to bed and songs to sing when you read the Bible; songs to sing at morning, noon, evening and midnight!

Finally, we get to the last few sections, which provide songs of response to God for other situations we may find ourselves in: songs that describe the Christian life as a pilgrimage, a race and warfare; songs for times of affliction—poverty, persecution, temptation, sickness and bereavement; then some songs for particular occasions—fasting days, funerals, prayer nights, New Year's, meetings for the poor and missionary meetings. There's even a little section of songs for the backslider!

When I look at a 150-year-old collection of worship songs like this, I'm inspired and encouraged to press on and take my songwriting a little more seriously. The Church needs songs that help us respond to God in worship as we walk out our lives before Him; songs that get to grips with all the wonderful facets of His nature, character and splendor; songs that provide an entry point for the person who doesn't know Him; songs that respond to, revere and call upon the Holy Spirit, who with the Father and Son is worshipped and glorified. There are so many more ways I can respond to my God in song.

Let's build up a greater vocabulary of songs so that we might more worthily magnify His name and more capably serve God's Church as lead worshippers.

the one thing...

(DARLENE ZSCHECH)

The one thing I'm increasingly aware of is the spiritual responsibility given to us by our Lord and King. He has trusted us with this season in history. We need to grow up as leaders in the things of God—not easily shaken, and immovable in our pursuit of bringing heaven to Earth. Lead worshippers who bring faith and annihilate fear. Who bring dancing and tread on mourning. Who bring courage and break down discouragement—in Spirit and truth—for the glory of God.

UNDERSTANDING WORSHIP

(PART 1)

CHRIS JACK

Reasons for Worship

Christians all do it. Sometimes we enjoy it. Often we don't—if we're really honest about it. Why do we bother? What's the point? Is there something better we could be doing with our time?

We're talking about worship, of course. It's a subject that frequently gives rise to heated debate, for we all have our preferences; we all know just how it should be done—and how it shouldn't! In this, as in many other areas of life, we know what we like, what appeals to us, what suits our tastes. And there is plenty to choose from: traditional, contemporary, liturgical, charismatic, alternative, blended—seemingly something for everyone. As the song goes, "I did it my way."

But what happens when *my way* isn't *your way*, and we're both in the same congregation? Tensions develop. Factions emerge. And before you know it, you are in a war zone. The phrase now used to describe this kind of situation is "Worship wars." Sadly, such wars are common in our day, causing much disruption and at times real hurt in our churches. Battles rage around musical preferences.

But is this really what it's all about? In our focus on *how* we worship, maybe we've missed the boat. Don't we first need to think about *what* worship is and *why* we worship? Surely it is only as we understand the *what* and the *why* of worship that we can properly begin to address the *how*; yet we persist with our disputes over styles of worship as though this is what matters most. In truth, much of the time we merely defend our personal preferences, however much we might endeavor to clothe our arguments in suitable theological garb.

As Constance Cherry stated:

Confusion abounds in our postmodern world concerning the nature of Christian worship.[1]

Biblically, worship is all about responding in right ways to God. And the first thing that we must grasp is that worship is primarily about God. While we may pay lip service readily to this fact, in practice it is often quite difficult for us to engage in. We live in a very self-centered world, where self-gratification, self-satisfaction, self-fulfillment and the like drive so much of our activity and determine so many of our responses. If we're not careful, we'll find ourselves evaluating our worship in this self-focused way. Of course, worship involves me; I am a participant in it. Yet it is not primarily about me or for me.

There are three key biblical reasons for worship. Note the significant fact that all are God-focused.

1. **God deserves our worship.** Worship is a right and fitting response to God both because of who He is and because of what He has done. This is a constant motif throughout Scripture, finding particular expression in the Psalms (see Pss. 98; 100; 104; 111). We worship God, then, in His infinite greatness and goodness, recognizing His superiority to us in every way; and we worship Him for His great acts as Creator and Redeemer. Something of this is vividly portrayed in Revelation 4—5, which

affords a glorious glimpse of the true worship taking place in heaven.

2. **God requires our worship.** The relationship between God and His people, under both the Old and the New Covenants, is established by God's initiative and on God's terms. In the Old Testament, the Law given at Sinai is in effect a statement of the terms of the Covenant. Within this statement is enshrined the command to worship God. It is implicit in the Ten Commandments (see Exod. 20:1-6) and made explicit elsewhere (see Exod. 23:25; Deut. 6:13; Matt. 4:10). And in the New Testament there is no less focus on worship as a Covenant requirement (see John 4:22-24; Rom. 12:1; Heb. 12:28). Furthermore, God's New Covenant people are described as a "royal priesthood" whose very calling is to "declare the praises" of God (1 Pet. 2:9). So worship is a requirement, a duty (and therefore, something to be done irrespective of how we *feel*, as a response of our will), as well as a natural and fitting response to God, which flows spontaneously from our minds and our hearts. Either way, it is about Him and for Him!

3. **God enables our worship.** Finally, it's worth noting that worship is only possible because God has made it so. It is He who decisively revealed Himself throughout the Old Testament and who has finalized that revelation in the person of His Son, Jesus Christ (see John 1:18). And it is He who, in Christ, has opened up a new basis for relationship with Himself (see 2 Cor. 5:17-21), offering direct access into His presence (see Eph. 2:18; Heb. 10:19-22). The remarkable thing is that on the basis of Christ's once-for-all sacrifice of Himself, God accepts our worship and even delights in it (see Rom. 12:1; Phil. 4:18). What is important to underline here is that worship, in all its forms and expressions, is first and foremost for God's pleasure, not ours.

> WHEN WE WORSHIP GOD FOR THE RIGHT REASONS, THE RESULT IS THAT WE CAN TRULY ENJOY HIM AS HE INTENDS WE SHOULD.

The remarkable irony is that when we get this perspective right—when we worship God for the right reasons, on His terms and as He has enabled us to—the result is that we can truly enjoy Him as He intends we should. Notwithstanding the exclusive language, this extract from the *Westminster Shorter Catechism* (written in the seventeenth century) still holds as a poignantly succinct statement of why we should worship God:

> What is the chief end of man? Man's chief end is to glorify God, and to enjoy him forever.[2]

It is what we were made for.

the one thing...

BRIAN DOERKSEN

Worship is an act of love; the great thing is that no two people express love in exactly the same way. How has God made you to express love? That's where the power will be!

creative insight

WHERE ARE GOD'S CELEBRITY CHEFS?

DAVID SALMON

When it comes to learning about worship, most of us head straight to the Psalms for some inspiration. But let me ask you this: Does your church overhead ever project the words from some of the more "difficult" Psalms? There are plenty straight-down-the-line "Praise the Lord" style of Psalms of course, but what do you do when you stumble across a rant from some disgruntled priest in Psalm 73? Why the story about ships being wrecked at sea in Psalm 107, and why the catalog of failures from Israel's past in Psalm 106?

The Psalms weren't just the ballads of self-indulgent songwriters, never to be heard in public. They were as much part of the Temple worship as the more famous songs of praise, like Psalm 150. And the truth is, the psalmists knew something that we in the twenty-first century often overlook: Truth that seeps out from the cracks of stories is absorbed deeper into the human heart than truth told as objective fact. What we glean from between the lines of all we see around us can have a deeply profound effect upon us.

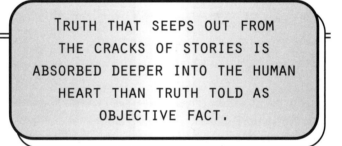

TRUTH THAT SEEPS OUT FROM THE CRACKS OF STORIES IS ABSORBED DEEPER INTO THE HUMAN HEART THAN TRUTH TOLD AS OBJECTIVE FACT.

A quick scan through the Bible shows that God seems to have chosen this way to communicate His truth to us. Between the two covers we find stories, histories, allegories, poetry, a play, ballads, transcripts of historical letters and wildly symbolic, visionary prose. God, throughout the Old Testament, spoke to the prophets in pictures, painting rich images of deep revelation. Jesus, when surrounded by an attentive audience, spoke in parables. He never spelled out the truth; rather, He contextualized it into stories that all could understand. Even today, through the Holy Spirit, we're given pictures and symbols that communicate truth to us. It seems to run in the family—a kind of Father, Son and Holy Spirit thing, a Trinity of storytellers. Learning through interpreting the world around us is built into the very way God has made us to be. We even dream in symbols.

Absorbing Nutrients

We take in truths the same way we take in nutrients—extracted and absorbed naturally from the food we eat. Yet, as a Church, we are so concerned about exactly what nutrients we need that we often forget what the meal should actually taste like. Our theological scientists in their research seminaries have spent years analyzing the things we eat, distilling them down to their constituent parts and then labeling them in systematic test tubes. It's vital that they do this, because without their tireless work we wouldn't have such a clear idea of what is needed for a good healthy diet. On the other hand, if it was left to them to come up with the menu, we would end up with a plateful of pills and tablets instead of, say, braised salmon fillet wrapped in prosciutto with herbs, on a bed of spinach and yogurt.

The repercussions of taking in nutrients this way actually go further than simply creating more appetizing meals. An iron supplement may be of some good; but iron, if taken in by eating foods like spinach or tuna, is actually absorbed into the body more efficiently. Nutritionists will tell you that a fresh orange—as well as looking and tasting fantastic—is a lot better for you than a vitamin C tablet.

Creating an Appetite

The restaurant needs the creativity of its chefs; the Church needs the creativity of its communicators to work skillfully with the ingredients it has—crafting images, inventing stories, telling parables, writing songs and painting pictures. These are the layered creations out of which seep the liberating truths of love and grace, the difficult truths of judgment and holiness and the deep paradoxes that make up our lives with God.

The wonderful thing about truth in this context is that it always speaks in a language your soul can understand. It will never violate your free will; and though it may challenge and confront, ultimately the choice is left to you. As Jesus said, "He who has ears, let him hear" (Matt. 11:15). When asked by His disciples why He told stories, Jesus replied, "Whenever someone has a ready heart for this, the insights and understandings flow freely. But if there is no readiness, any trace of receptivity soon disappears. That's why I tell stories: to create readiness, to nudge the people toward receptive insight" (Matt. 13:11-13, *THE MESSAGE*).

If Jesus spoke to the crowds this way, should we not work hard at following His example? We live among a generation of people who want nothing to do with the Church. Listen to them for long, and you will discover that it's not so much the message they dislike, as much as the way they are told it. The world has had enough of being force-fed pills; yet it remains in desperate need of the divine nutrients, vitamins and minerals of which it has been starved for so long.

Is it because we fear we might miss some vital nutrients that we have lost sight of the meal through which these truths are most effectively absorbed into the body? Do we not trust the chefs? The answer is to embrace the theologians and to give freedom to the artists. As coworkers with Christ, we must learn to dwell together in the same camp and realize just how much we need each other.

The Bridegroom is calling all of mankind to His banqueting table, but where are His celebrity chefs?

the one thing...

MATT REDMAN

Sometimes it can be tempting to strive to do something *significant*. We find ourselves wanting to write a significant song that will touch many hearts or lead a significant time of worship in which lives are truly changed. But we are not called to significance. Instead, the calling is to *obedience*. Look through the Bible and see how obedience reaps some major, significant outcomes. Look at Moses or Noah for example. Ultimately, look at Jesus and the Cross. The most significant act in all of history was one of sheer, humble, enduring obedience.

Whether we're called to be up in front or behind the scenes, obedience is always significant in the eyes of God.

searching the psalms

REFLECTIONS ON PSALM 8

(PART 2)

Louie Giglio

A Life of Consideration

When I consider . . . what is man?

PSALM 8:3-4

Somewhere between these two phrases worship begins.

The life of worship is a life of consideration. In other words, creating time and space to think is essential for developing a lifestyle of God-sized worship. A life of consideration requires time to wonder. Time to dwell. Time to ponder. Time to look up.

The psalmist had plenty of time to consider. I guess you could say it was one of the fringe benefits of being a herder of sheep. His office was shrouded by a huge sky. His nightly entertainment was the dancing heavens above. Alone and awake, he had lots of time to look up and wonder. Grasping at the endless universe above made his head spin. Looking up, he said, "When I consider your heavens, the work of your fingers, the moon and the stars, which you have set in place, what is man that you are mindful of him?" (Ps. 8:3-4).

Looking up is what worship is all about, especially for those of us who spend most of our time looking around. Have you ever noticed that when we look around at our circumstances, they tend to deflate worship, not inspire it? Looking around we see frustration. We see unfinished tasks. We see imperfection and injustice. Disease. We also see a multitude of lesser gods.

But when we look up, everything changes. Intrigued by the night sky, David saw order. Looking up, he was confronted with the Incomprehensible. The Eternal. The Mysterious. The Expansive. The Beautiful. He saw forever black and brilliant light. On the darkest of nights, the stars seemed to stoop to touch him. The blacker the night, the brighter they glowed. The more isolated his location, the closer they appeared.

And how they sang!

Someone made us, fancy that!
And He knows us each by name.
Here we hover, countless counted,
spoken here to tell His fame.
Stretch your mind, reach around us,
though it's difficult we know.
Stand in awe, drink in the wonder,
join and sing our Maker's praise.

O LORD, our Lord, how majestic is your name in
all the earth! (Ps. 8:1).

> FOR EACH OF US WORSHIP BEGINS
> AS WE INTENTIONALLY CREATE
> ENOUGH SPACE TO LOOK UP.

For each of us worship begins as we intentionally create enough space to look up. No, it's not imperative that
you spend a night alone with sheep. But it is essential that
you take a deep breath and allow your thoughts to drift
from what is made to the One who makes it. We must take
time to consider God.

Looking up, two things happen: God gets bigger and we get smaller. David wonders aloud, "What is man that you are mindful of him?" (Ps. 8:4). That's the question we ask when we take time to consider. Instantly resized, we marvel at the wonder of it all. Seeing God arrayed in uncontainable splendor, we robe ourselves in humility, floored that we matter at all.

Nonconsiderers (I think I just invented that term) star in their own little universes, barely stopping to notice that their entire world—and all that captivates them—could easily fit on the head of the smallest of pins. But those who look up soon realize that they are in fact quite tiny, amazed that a God so big cares for them, who are so small.

You see, David was looking up in amazement while at the same time having a conversation with the Architect of all he could see. I can hear him saying, "What? Me, talking to You? How's that? I mean, who am I that I should even matter to You."

But it's true. This ageless Creator has called us by name, too, making us a little lower than the heavenly beings, crowning us with glory and honor and making us to rule over the work of His hands (see Ps. 8:5-6).

Once again David feels so small. But it's a good small, not a bad small. In fact, it's a glorious small; it causes him to embrace his true value in the arms of a loving God, propelling him to offer unrestrained glory to the Maker of all things. As Andrew Murray writes:

> It is only in the possession of God that I lose myself. As it is in the height and breadth and glory of the sunshine that the littleness of a speck of dust playing in the sunlight is seen, so humility is our being, in God's presence, nothing but a speck dwelling in the sunlight of His love. . . . How great is God! How small am I! Lost, swallowed up in Love's immensity! God only there, not I.[1]

There's a big, big God up there who knows your name—just a little something for your consideration.

the one thing...

BRENTON BROWN

The one thing I would say is to never stop God from working on your heart just because you're up the front leading people in worship.

We often start out on this journey like a broken-down car in need of repair. Most of us want to get the car totally sorted and fixed before we start the journey. But God says, "Start the journey anyway; you'll find the service stations and mechanics on the way." As we continue on the way into Him, periodically He pulls us aside and services us, making us more and more like His Son. That's how this God-life works. But there's a real temptation when we become leaders to think that simply because we're at the front leading, our motors are all sorted out and we don't need any more fixing. Of course that's not true. Leadership might mean we get to learn some of our lessons out front in public, but it is never an excuse to stop learning and growing.

THE CROSS

DON WILLIAMS

Exploring All Angles

For the ancient world, crucifixion was the ultimate penalty. It included torture as well as capital punishment. To haul the cross to the place of execution and to hang naked, broken and bleeding were shameful enough. Then to die of suffocation—no longer able to support the body's weight on nailed hands or wrists—was horror in life, relieved only by death. No wonder the Romans called the cross the fatal wood, the infamous stake, the extreme penalty. In general, no citizen could be crucified. This death was reserved for the punishment of slaves, aliens and outlaws. Legal terror contributed to Rome's obsession

with controlling her far-flung empire. Now we understand why Paul says that the Word of the Cross is folly to
the Greeks and a scandal to the Jews (see 1 Cor. 1:23).
When he claims not to be ashamed of the gospel (see
Rom. 1:16), he has every right to be. The Word of the
Cross, Jesus Christ and Him crucified, is offensive for at
least four reasons.

First, it is culturally offensive. No one speaks of the
Cross in polite society. That God, eternal and immutable,
could be crucified is crazy. Second, it is historically offensive. Christians claim that a peasant, itinerant Jew, legally
and brutally executed under Roman law, is the Lord of the
universe and the Savior of the world. He alone deserves the
exalted titles carried by the emperor. Third, it is philosoph-
ically offensive. This is the offense of the particular. Rather
than the Cross, at best, being an illustration of divine love,
it is the basis for divine love. This particular Cross estab-
lishes God's universal mercy and forgiveness for all.
Fourth, it is morally offensive. To put it simply: You cannot
save yourself. Salvation is only by faith in the crucified
Jesus, atoning once for all for sin. The mangled Messiah is
both God incarnate and the risen, reigning Lord.

With these offenses, why did the earliest Christians
glory in the Cross? Wouldn't they downplay it for the
sake of relevance, winning the right to be heard? Why did

they hold this bloody instrument up before the gaping ancient world?

THE CENTER OF THE NEW TESTAMENT

The heart of the New Testament is not the ethic of Jesus or the example of Jesus or the wisdom of Jesus or even the suffering service of Jesus. The heart of the New Testament is the Cross, seen now through the lens of the risen, exalted Lord. Martin Kahler, in an overstatement, calls our four Gospels "passion narratives with an introduction."[1] Each one moves resolutely to Jesus' final week in Jerusalem: the

> THE HEART OF THE NEW TESTAMENT IS THE CROSS, SEEN NOW THROUGH THE LENS OF THE RISEN, EXALTED LORD.

plot against His life; His meal with His disciples, establishing the New Covenant in His body and blood; his arrest; His trial; His execution (described in detail); and His resurrection from the dead. All the preaching in the book of Acts drives to the Cross (and the resurrection and reign of Jesus). Paul tells the Corinthians that he determined to "know nothing while I was with you except Jesus Christ and him crucified" (1 Cor. 2:2). Hebrews 9 presents Jesus as our great high priest who has gone, not into the Jerusalem Temple, but into heaven itself, bearing not animal blood but His own blood, making a once-for-all atonement for sin. Peter calls slaves to follow the example of Jesus, based on the sacrificial death of the servant in Isaiah 53 (see 1 Pet. 2:21-25). John writes, "This is love: not that we loved God, but that he loved us and sent his Son as an atoning sacrifice for our sins" (1 John 4:10). The book of Revelation shows the Lamb who was slain as the Lord of the universe. His blood purchased us for God (see Rev. 5:9).

THE WORDS OF SALVATION

In *The Apostolic Preaching of the Cross*, Leon Morris traces the Old Testament, classical and Jewish backgrounds of the New Testament words of salvation. Here are his conclusions:

1. **Redemption:** to set free from slavery, with the payment of a substitutionary price. "Instead of our death there is His, instead of our slavery there is His blood."[2]

2. **Covenant:** God's unilateral agreement to bind

Himself to us through the death of His Son. "The new covenant is essentially a covenant based upon divine forgiveness of sin [through the blood of Jesus]."[3]

3. **The Blood:** Life poured out or given up in death. "The blood which atones is that which flows when the death penalty is inflicted on the criminal [or the substitute who dies in his place]."[4]

4. **Propitiation:** "Where there is sin, there is wrath."[5] We cannot remove divine wrath by placating it. God does it by taking His own wrath upon Himself in the death of His Son.

5. **Reconciliation:** "It is God's demand for holiness which causes the enmity [against mankind's sin]."[6] God takes His enmity (wrath) upon Himself in His Son. The war is over; peace has come.

6. **Justification:** Christ, the righteous one, dies for the unrighteous, bearing their judgment in His death, so that we may be acquitted or justified before God by faith in Him. In the death of Christ, God proves Himself to be just (sin's penalty is paid) and the justifier of those who have faith in Jesus (see Rom. 3:26). "Even the

act of forgiveness which might be thought of as an act of mercy was seen to be also an act in accordance with righteousness. The very act wherein He delivers men is one in which He shows Himself to be acting righteously. . . . Righteousness . . . is a status conferred on men by God on the grounds of the atoning work of Christ."[7] By faith, they will stand before Him not guilty on the day of judgment.

THE STORY OF SALVATION

Tom Wright teaches us that the Exodus is "the controlling narrative of the Bible."[8] In Israel's deliverance two things happen: First, God's people are set free from slavery to Pharaoh and the gods of Egypt. Second, they are set free from the wrath of God. When the final plague—the death of the firstborn—falls on Egypt, Israel is subject to the same plague. But God provides a substitute. Each household is to sacrifice a lamb and mark the door with its blood. When the angel of death comes, seeing the blood, it passes over. Salvation, then, is to be deliverance both from bondage and from the wrath of God.

When we fast-forward to the New Testament, we see that Jesus comes to bring the final exodus. He sets us free, not from slavery to Egypt or Rome (or any other political power), but from slavery to Satan and his kingdom of darkness. Proclaiming the kingdom of God, He sweeps through Israel casting out demons and healing the sick. Then, as Paul says, Jesus disarms the demonic powers on the cross (see Col. 2:14-15). When He lifts the judgment of the law from us, He takes away Satan's power to accuse us and hold us in bondage.

Jesus also comes to set us free from the wrath of God against our sin. He is our Passover Lamb (see 1 Cor. 5:7). His blood protects us. On the cross, He cries, "My God, my God, why have you forsaken me?" (Mark 15:34). As Helmut Thielicke says, "In the cross there is a pain in God's heart."[9] The Forsaken is also forgiving, pleading on our behalf, "Father, forgive them, for they do not know what they are doing" (Luke 23:34). His death ends in triumph—not "I am finished" but "It is finished" (John 19:30). The work of atonement is done. Divine justice is satisfied. God now forgives sinners freely through His Son.

THE EXPLORATION OF ALL ANGLES

Throughout history, Christians have thought about the Cross from a variety of perspectives. These are often called theories of the atonement; but it is better to call them angles on the atonement, because we will never understand fully what Christ has done for us on the cross. Each angle carries some truth. Here are three: First, there is the cosmic angle. On the cross, Jesus defeated Satan. The devil thought he had killed God's Son, but—in a metaphor of the Early Church fathers—Jesus was the bait and the Cross the hook that reeled in our enemy. All the demonic power to afflict, infest, accuse and condemn is triumphed over in the Cross (and in the resurrection of Jesus from the dead).

Second, there is the human angle. The Cross reveals us. It scandalizes us. It rips us apart. All self-justification dies here. We have executed the Son of God.

> When I survey the wondrous cross On which the Prince of glory died, My richest gain I count but loss, And pour contempt on all my pride.

But the Cross reveals the depth of God's love at the same time. As we see Jesus' sacrifice, we are changed.

> Were the whole realm of nature mine, That were a present far too small: Love so amazing, so divine, Demands my soul, my life, my all.[10]

Third, and more mysteriously, there is the divine angle. The Cross is God's work for Himself before it is His work for us. In the Cross, He reconciles His justice and His mercy. As Luther says, holiness and love kiss in the Cross.

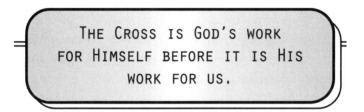

THE CROSS IS GOD'S WORK FOR HIMSELF BEFORE IT IS HIS WORK FOR US.

As Jesus dies in the place of sinners, divine justice is satisfied and divine mercy is extended. What changes is not God's heart to forgive us but the ground upon which He may do so.[11]

FINAL THOUGHT

James Denney writes that if we were sitting on the end of a pier and a man crying, "I love you, I love you," were to come running down the pier and jump into the swirling waters and be carried away, we would think he is crazy. But if we were sitting on the end of a pier and were to fall into the swirling waters and were being carried away, and a man crying, "I love you, I love you," were to run down the pier and jump into the waters, throw his arms around us and pull us out, we would be eternally grateful.[12] This is what Jesus has done for us as we are drowning in sin and judgment. Here is our debt to Him: We are eternally grateful and must express this at the heart of worship.

In these times, it is so important that worship leaders and worship songwriters get to grips with the Cross. It is the centerpiece of our faith, and as such, we must explore every angle of this wondrous, powerful Cross.

the one thing...

WAYNE DRAIN

I strongly encourage you to find a pastor or an older brother or sister in the Lord whom you can trust and to whom you can be accountable.

We are very privileged to do what we do as songwriters, artists or worship leaders. We often get much more attention than we either deserve or need. With this attention can come temptations such as pride or unfaithfulness. We need someone in our lives who will love us and encourage us in our giftings but who will not become so enamored with us that they can't speak honestly into our lives.

"Accountability" is not a four-letter word. It doesn't mean to be controlled in an abusive manner. It means to be liable, to be called to account. Hebrews 13:17 tells us that we should obey our leaders and submit to their authority, for they keep watch over us as those who must give an account. "Obey" is a four-letter word. But it's a good one! It means to adapt. Accountability will help us adapt ourselves to the character of Christ as we seek to become more like Him in all we do.

creative insight

THE REAL WORSHIP LEADER

MATT REDMAN

The Holy Spirit of God is the ultimate worship leader. In Philippians 3:3, we're reminded that we "worship by the Spirit of God." He is the agent and orchestrator of our worship. Nothing meaningful, spiritual or true happens in worship without Him. We become lead worshippers, setting an example for others to follow, while listening out for the essential prompting of the Holy Spirit.

There are some pretty big implications for us when we explore this view of the Holy Spirit's being the ultimate worship leader. First, it releases us from some pressure. When we see Him as the worship leader, we realize more than ever that we can't *make* worship happen. We can't hype it or conjure it up out of nowhere. Worship is always birthed by the Holy Spirit.

At the same time, this view keeps us dependent. We have a responsibility to make sure we're putting ourselves in the best possible place to hear those whisperings of the

> WHEN WE SEE THE HOLY SPIRIT AS THE WORSHIP LEADER, WE REALIZE MORE THAN EVER THAT WE CAN'T *MAKE* WORSHIP HAPPEN.

Holy Spirit. We're totally dependent on Him for the next step. I once heard Ken Gire use the analogy of a dance with the Lord. You don't necessarily have to know the end of the dance; you just have to follow His lead, step-by-step. Dependence is a vulnerable position, but as Oswald Chambers once said, "Weakness and dependence will always be the occasion for the Spirit of God to manifest His power."[1]

In reality, no matter how many years of experience we have, we're just as dependent as the first time we ever led. We might be better singers now or know a few more chords—and these things are genuinely helpful—yet the most vital factor hasn't changed at all: We need the Holy

Spirit to help us lead, just as much as we ever did. He has no substitute or replacement. Formulas, experience, worship models and tried-and-tested songs will only take us so far. The Holy Spirit will always take us deeper.

If we take this view of worship leading, then before long we realize that not everything needs to originate from up front. This is a huge implication. We can get so used to everything's being led from the stage, but we must not assume that the Holy Spirit wants to lead the whole time of worship in song through only one person. Songs can start from within the congregation, too. This is scary, yes, but that is part of being dependent.

We'll even find ourselves praying differently before meetings. Rather than asking, "Lord, anoint the musicians, the singers and the worship leader," the priority in prayer becomes, "God, come and anoint Your people to worship You as we gather today." A subtle shift, yet a momentous one.

There is of course a real value in having a lead worshipper up front—someone who's gifted in helping us travel together and who has thoughtfully prayed for some sense of direction. So, there's no need to fire anybody. Just a little change of approach—more space to be led afresh by other members of the congregation, as they sense the Holy Spirit's leading.

Sometimes we get carried away and forget that in the end, the music is primarily a tool (a beautiful tool, no question) to help us express our worship together. This shift of emphasis, to see the Holy Spirit as worship leader, strongly reminds us that we are involved here in a spiritual encounter and not just a musical one.

Real worship will always be a spiritual event, so let us seek to follow the prompting of the real worship leader, the Holy Spirit.

the one thing...

ANDREW PHILIP

We are always learning to listen. First, to God, because He has spoken to us; and if we are to respond appropriately in worship, we must make every effort to hear Him accurately. Second, to the world, because we are called to show mercy; and how are we to do that unless we hear its cries for help? And last, to one another in the Church, because we all still carry our brokenness; and if we are to live in liberty, we need to bear with one another in love (see Eph. 4:2).

This is the context of our lives—the context in which we are living as we gather to worship. Our listening begins long before we pick up an instrument and extends far deeper than merely trying to keep time and play in the right key. Our listening—to God and to one another—forms the shape of our lives. And it is the shape of our lives that determines whether what we do when we gather on a Sunday morning is an expression of worship—something that truly brings God glory—or an expression of our selfishness, or disunity. God hears our hearts far more loudly than He does the sounds we make.

SKILL AND SENSITIVITY

LES MOIR

In the first few verses of Psalm 33, we're urged to make music to the Lord, sing to Him a new song and play skillfully. The word "skillfully" here means two things. First, we're to be the best that we can be on our instruments—as practiced and prepared as possible. And second, we need to learn how to play sensitively, with an ability to flow with the Holy Spirit in our times of congregational worship.

Musicians may have great technique, but without this sensitivity they will often distract from, rather than add to, the worship time. This sensitivity leads us to play the right thing at the right time. Eric Clapton once said that his ambition was to make people cry by playing just one note![1] Sometimes less is actually more.

In 1 Chronicles 25 we read about the Levite priests who took care of the worship in the Temple and who were "trained and skilled in music for the LORD" (v. 7). We

> # TAKE LESSONS, STUDY, PUSH YOURSELF—AND LEARN TO GET INTO THE GROOVE WITH GOD.

sense here a dedication to their calling, and so it should be with us. Whatever we do, we should work at it with all of our hearts, spending time developing our gifting and learning to improve our playing as an expression of our love to Him. Take lessons, study, push yourself—learn different scales and chords, as well as chord shapes—and learn to get into the groove with God. As trumpet player and vocalist Phil Driscoll once commented, "I am trying to keep my craft at a level that will allow me to flow with the Holy Sprit."[2]

As musicians, we can express the heart of God through our playing. Music is a language that God speaks through, just as God spoke through the rest of creation. And the more we learn, the greater the vocabulary we'll have available to express what God is saying.

Be alert, as you never know where the Holy Spirit will lead. Let your worship be more than songs—but use the songs as a launchpad into something new. For example, in times of intercession God may want you to express His heart for a nation with the sound of that culture, so learn to play other styles—or even indigenous instruments—and be ready.

In times of worshipping as a team, it's great to express worship to God together, but there may come a time and dynamic when you will feel prompted by the Holy Spirit to play out. So spend time improvising, singing out new songs and making melody to God. And remember, anything that can be spoken can be sung.

One weekend we had a worship seminar, and I asked the musicians if they felt anything from the Lord. One of the bass players said he was feeling God's joy bubbling up. I handed him my bass, and he started to play a funky bass figure. Soon the drummer and the whole band joined in, and then everyone started to dance. Everyone there experienced the joy of the Lord in that moment.

I'm also reminded of being inspired by a violinist, Ruth Fazal, who would play out while Scripture was read aloud. She seemed to be able to convey the meaning of each verse as it was being read.

In the Old Testament, we see musicians being · release the prophetic word. In 2 Kings 3:14, Elisha a a harpist to be brought, and while the harpist is playing, the hand of the Lord came upon him and he prophesied. We also see deliverance, as in the case of David playing before Saul: "David would take his harp and play. Then relief would come to Saul; . . . and the evil spirit would leave him" (1 Sam. 16:23).

As musicians, we need to have one ear listening to the worship leader and the musicians, and the other ear listening to what the Holy Spirit is saying and doing. Let's work at this and learn to flow with the Holy Spirit.

In the Old Testament there is an abundance of worship language. This language shows something of the variety and extent of Old Testament worship: its different forms and expressions, its personal and communal dimensions and its ordinary and extraordinary phenomena. From this we learn what worship is and how it should be offered.

There are three main Hebrew words used in the Old Testament for "worship"—that is, three words which are regularly translated "worship" in English versions of the Bible. In short, the biblical terminology shows that worship is

- submission,
- service, and
- reverence.

Significantly, all three have direct parallels in the Greek of the New Testament. What this means—and it is worth underlining at the outset—is that there is considerable consistency and continuity between the Old Testament's understanding of worship and that of the New Testament. Certainly, there are differences of content and form. However, in terms of the basic understanding of what worship is and what it involves, there is a strongly unified picture which runs right through the Bible.

Each of these keywords provides important foundations for our understanding of what worship is. In point of fact, each conveys a different aspect of the complex, multifaceted activity we call worship.

> The biblical words for worship do not represent discrete concepts but are part of a whole mosaic of thought about the way to relate to God. They are important windows into that structure of thought.[2]

The first "window," and the most common word for worship in the Old Testament, is the Hebrew word *hawah*. The actual form of the word is *hishtahawah*, and it means to bow down, do obeisance, pay homage and, of course, worship. Of the 170 occurrences of hawah, just under half (approximately 75) are translated "worship" in the *New International Version*. Around the same number are rendered "bow down," with the simple "bow" in several cases. In six passages the phrase "pay honor" is used, and "pay homage" is used once.

Bowing down is clearly a vital component of the meaning of the word. This physical gesture was common within the culture of the times. Bowing was a way of honoring someone, a mark of respect. It could also indicate submission, especially when performed in the presence of a figure of authority.

The important thing in all this is the intent behind the gesture. Of course, like any gesture, it could (and can) be performed superficially, even hypocritically. Action and

> "HAWAH" CONVEYS THE IDEA OF HONORING GOD AND EXPRESSING AN ATTITUDE OF SUBMISSION TO HIM.

attitude must go hand in hand, so as a word for worship, "hawah" conveys the idea of honoring God and expressing an attitude of submission to Him.

We turn next to the Greek word *proskuneo*. According to H. Schönweiss and C. Brown,

> among the Greeks the verb is a technical term for the adoration of the gods, meaning to fall down, prostrate oneself, adore on one's knees. In addition to the external act of prostrating oneself in worship, *proskuneo* can denote the corresponding inward attitude of reverence and humility.[3]

"Proskuneo" is the most common word for worship in the New Testament, just as "hawah" is in the Old Testament. Amongst other things, this enhances the sense of continuity between the two testaments. The primary idea behind the word is that of paying homage, honoring with a submissive spirit (and perhaps gesture) the One who is deemed to be worthy and superior. As with hawah, it is essentially a matter of an inward attitude that may be reflected in an outward gesture. In both meaning and usage the two words "hawah" and "proskuneo" are extremely close parallels.

The unity of outlook between the New Testament and the Old Testament is emphasized by the use of these parallel terms. This is important to grasp. The two testaments present a single, harmonious picture of the essentials of worship. There is a development between the Old Testament and New Testament in the areas of form and expression of worship; and in particular, there is in the New Testament the momentous and unique revelation of Jesus Christ with all its significance for worship. However, the essence of what worship is remains constant from Genesis to Revelation.

Looking at the first biblical word group (the parallel terms "hawah" and "proskuneo"), we are beginning to appreciate something of what the essence of worship is: humble submission to God.

The next biblical word group shows us that worship involves work or service. The relevant Hebrew term is *'abad*, and in all, it is found 289 times in the Old Testament. This verb can mean to work, to do and to perform as well as to serve and to worship. In the *New International Version* it is most frequently translated by the word "serve" (around 125 times). Quite often this is in contexts where God is the object of the verb, the one being served. The phrase "to serve the LORD [Yahweh]" is used 56 times. It is in such usage that the notion of worship is conveyed, even where translators opt for "serve" rather than "worship" (see Exod. 3:12; Deut. 10:12; Isa. 19:21).

As well as being employed in a variety of contexts where service of God is signified, "'abad" is also specifically used for religious service, including that related to the sacrificial system. (see Num. 3:7; 8:11). The whole sacrificial system, with its detailed rituals and apparatus, was given by God to enable His people, Israel, to serve (worship) Him in an appropriate manner.

Moving on to the New Testament, there are two Greek verbs that, together with a number of related words, convey the same essential idea as "'abad." They are *latreuo* and *leitourgeo*. "Latreuo" is found 21 times and means "to serve" or "to worship." It is translated in the *New International Version* as "worship" 8 times, "serve" 12 times and "minister" once.

All New Testament occurrences of "latreuo" are in religious contexts where the service offered is not to another human being but to God (see Luke 2:37; Acts 26:7; Phil. 3:3; Heb. 12:28). Although in the Septuagint (Greek translation of the Old Testament) the primary use of the word is in relation to the ceremonial worship of the sacrificial system, in the New Testament, other than in Hebrews, this becomes secondary.

The second Greek verb, "leitourgeo," occurs only three times in the New Testament (see Acts 13:2; Rom. 15:27; Heb. 10:11). Three other associated terms need to be noted: *leitourgia*, translated as "service" or "ministry" (six times); *leitourgikos*, "serving" or "ministering" (once); and *leitourgos*, "servant" or "minister" (five times).

In its range of meaning, "leitourgeo" is very close to "latreuo." However, its distinctive is that in the Septuagint it is used almost exclusively for the service of priests and Levites in the Temple. It effectively functions as a technical term for that service. In the New Testament usage of the word group, this cultic association is preserved at times, particularly in Hebrews, where comparisons between the Old Covenant and the New Covenant are being made (see Luke 1:23; Heb. 9:21; 10:11). But at other times a noncultic service is denoted (see Phil. 2:25,30)

Worship, then, is service of God expressed, not only in religious gatherings, but also in every area of life. It is worth reflecting on the fact that we refer to many of our meetings as services. That is not inappropriate in the light

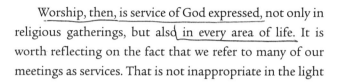

WORSHIP IS SERVICE OF GOD EXPRESSED, NOT ONLY IN RELIGIOUS GATHERINGS, BUT ALSO IN EVERY AREA OF LIFE.

of the insight received through this second biblical window into worship. We might do well to ponder, however, how far our *services* embody true *service* of God!

We now complete our survey of the main biblical vocabulary for worship, looking through our third window to see that worship is fear or reverence of God. The Hebrew word *yare'* is found over 300 times in the Old Testament. In the vast majority of instances it is translated in the *New International Version* as "afraid," "fear" or another associated term. In approximately 80 percent of the passages in which the verb is found, the object of fear is God. The concept of the fear of the Lord features strongly in the Old Testament, especially in the wisdom books. Usually, such fear is not to be understood as terror or dread but as a heightened attitude of awe or respect.

On occasion, the *New International Version* translates "yare'" as "worship"—15 times in all (Judg. 6:10; 1 Kings 18:12; 2 Kings 17:7,25,28,32,34,35,36,37,38,39,41; Isa. 29:13; Jon. 1:9). By contrast, it is only so translated once in the *Revised Standard Version* (Josh. 22:25). Interestingly, the one place where the *Revised Standard Version* translators opted for "worship," the *New International Version* has "fear." Conversely, in 1 Kings 18:12 the *Revised Standard Version* has "revere" for the *New International Version*'s "worship." Once again we note the flexibility of translation possibilities.

But we may conclude that when used with reference to worship, "yare'" emphasizes the idea of awe of or reverent respect for God.

> Worship as reverent obedience marked the practical outworking of the fear of God in the life of the community of faith—formally in proper religious service . . . and informally in right living.[4]

Andrew Hill rightly emphasizes the implications of the attitude of fear or reverence of God in terms of obedience. As the Old Testament wisdom literature especially makes clear, the fear of the Lord consists of a way of life that cor-

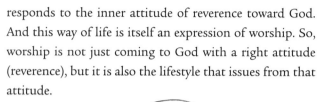

responds to the inner attitude of reverence toward God. And this way of life is itself an expression of worship. So, worship is not just coming to God with a right attitude (reverence), but it is also the lifestyle that issues from that attitude.

The New Testament equivalent of "yare'" is *sebomai*. It is used a number of times in the Septuagint for "yare'" (see Job 1:9; Isa. 29:13; Jon. 1:9). "Sebomai" occurs 10 times in the New Testament. It means to revere, to worship or to be devout; it is translated as "worship" 6 times in the *New International Version* (Matt. 15:9; Mark 7:7; Acts 16:14; 18:7,13; 19:27). Other occurrences are translated in the *New International Version* as "God-fearing" or "devout" (see Acts 13:43,50; 17:4,17). A number of related terms are found in the New Testament.

As with both word groups already studied, the New Testament once again confirms a perspective on worship first introduced in the Old Testament. This time it is that of worship as reverence of God—reverence that involves the dimension of awe. Our God is awesome! He is awesome in His greatness, His majesty and His holiness—to highlight a few key areas not always given their due place in our thinking and our worship today. Are these words of Tozer, first preached 40 years ago, perhaps even more true today?

I am finding that many Christians are really not comfortable with the holy attributes of God. In such cases I am forced to wonder about the quality of the worship they try to offer to him.[5]

There is one verse in the Old Testament which uses all three Hebrew words for worship that we have studied. The three windows into worship—submission, service and reverence—are all brought together in a single verse: 2 Kings 17:35. It is interesting to compare how different translations handle this verse. The *New International Version* reads:

> When the LORD made a covenant with the Israelites, he commanded them: "Do not worship [yare'] any other gods or bow down [hawah] to them, serve them ['abad] or sacrifice to them."

In the *Revised Standard Version* we read:

> The Lord made a covenant with them, and commanded them, "You shall not fear other gods or bow yourselves to them or serve them or sacrifice to them."

In principle, each of the words could be translated "worship"—"Do not worship . . . or worship . . . or worship"—though this would be rather flat and miss the nuances of the individual Hebrew words. Alternatively, as with the *Revised Standard Version*, the choice could be made to translate none of the words as "worship." Either way—or however else the words are rendered into English—the verse is concerned with worship. True, in this instance it is the

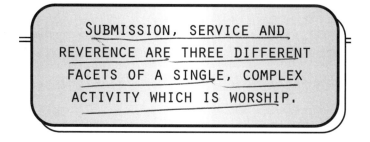

SUBMISSION, SERVICE AND REVERENCE ARE THREE DIFFERENT FACETS OF A SINGLE, COMPLEX ACTIVITY WHICH IS WORSHIP.

worship of other gods—worship which the Lord insists should not be offered. But what is not to be offered to other gods is to be offered to the one true God, as the next verse makes clear.

The important thing here is to understand that these three windows—submission, service, reverence— are not alternatives, representing three different forms of worship. Rather, they are three different facets of a single, complex activity which is worship, thus we begin to understand something of the nature of worship from a biblical perspective.

the one thing...

(R I T A   S P R I N G E R)

Sometimes when we see worship being modeled with great music and a wonderful sound, we look at the talent and don't realize that true worship often comes with a price tag. We tend to look for the end result and ignore the in-between stuff it takes to get us there.

Life brings us many circumstances and dreams, which sometimes come with a timetable and a box of patience. During those seasons, while we wait for release, we have a great opportunity to know Jesus more and let Him be known through us.

THOUGHTS ON SONGWRITING

(PART 2)

Crafting Lyrics

Write about scriptural principles that are underemphasized in contemporary worship songs.

Try to use as much nonreligious vocabulary as possible to paint a scripturally accurate picture of knowing and following God. Make sure the lyrics are more than just correct—they have to be compelling—and like a good sermon, they have to appeal to the mind and emotions.

Make sure your lyrics are universal and they apply to all Christians. The various facets of relationship with God and our response to God's personality and commands are universal. Not only should the content be universal, but the vocabulary you are using should relate to a broad spectrum of people, too. For example, avoid theological terms that will be unknown to some Christians and non-Christians. Instead, find creative ways to describe these terms in a fresh and personal way.

Andy Park

I am beginning to think that writing worship songs is far too important to leave to just the singers and musicians. For some reason, contemporary worship music seems to

> WRITING WORSHIP SONGS IS FAR TOO IMPORTANT TO LEAVE TO JUST THE SINGERS AND MUSICIANS.

have taken on board the rock-and-pop model of the singer-songwriter without questioning it and assumes that the singer-musician should be the one to write both the words and music of the song. Why?

I know we have some great songs around, but let's not be too easily satisfied. We need to get the theologians involved with the poets and lyricists, and get them all involved with the music writers. We mustn't be "precious" about all this.

Andy Piercy

Jesus says that "out of the overflow of the heart the mouth speaks" (Matt. 12:34). The heart is the main wellspring for lyrics. If what goes in is rich, then the fruit is likely to be rich. If what we are feeding on is shallow, then our lyrics become dry and uninspiring. We need to overflow from the Word of God. There is no substitute for the revelation God brings through His written word.

Be ruthless with your lyrics. Don't settle for lines that are second best. When it comes to putting song lyrics together, it's good to try to say things in a fresh way, avoiding overdone rhymes such as "You pour out Your grace, as I seek Your face." The real skill is presenting an old theme in a fresh and inspiring way.

Martyn Layzell

Songwriters are philosophers and should take their art and ministry seriously. What is written is pondered by the mind and many times received in the heart, affecting the listeners in the deep places of their hearts. Music combined with lyrics is a powerful force because the listener contemplates it and repeats it over and over.

We have a responsibility because of this to be God-centered and theologically sound. Songs are miniature injections into people or groups, so desire your injection to honor God.

Charlie Hall

The congregational lyric writer must have a pastoral heart. This writer need not necessarily be the greatest counselor or have the ultimate listening ear, but he or she must have a heart for the people of God. With every line of the song, let's remember our congregations. Never honor the music above the people. In other words, make every effort to write singable songs. In the same way, go out of your way to write lyrics that are easy for the congregation to understand and make their own. Too many times I've seen worship song lyrics that are so subjective and particular to the writers that no one singing them actually has a clue about what they mean. All this, done in the name of poetry. But people are more important than poetry. Yes, by all means be a poet, but first of all be a pastor.

Matt Redman

I think writing congregational song lyrics is something that we don't labor over as much as we should. It's very easy to write obvious lyrics using the classic clichés, but to write something fresh that really adds to a church's worship takes time and thought.

When writing a worship song, I always turn to the Bible to see what it says on the matter. But I've been trying to get beyond just simply copying down verses from the Bible and putting them in songs. Though that is a valid way to write Scripture songs, there's also something to be said for trying poetically to express these timeless truths in different ways. Some songs are even a mixture of many different parts of Scripture.

Lastly, we need to keep finding ways of expressing God's majesty and glory. Do our lyrics open eyes up to the greatness of God? Do they fill our minds and hearts with the glorious truth of who He is? They are the songs the Church needs to sing.

Tim Hughes

the one thing...

(TOMMY WALKER)

May the dream never die that someday when people want to go find the most moving and excellent art, they will go to the Church. I am so convinced that we've only just begun to tap into some of the improvisational sounds that can be created in the presence of God. These are the sounds the world can't touch yet will be drawn to.

Practical worship leading

CELL, CONGREGATION, CELEBRATION

MATT REDMAN

Worship Leading in Three Contexts

Jesse Owens, Carl Lewis, Michael Johnson—some of the greatest athletes ever known. But what makes them so remarkable? What distinguishes them from other great athletes of their time? In a word, versatility. Many athletes over the years have had victories in one track event or another. But much rarer is an athlete who can tackle more than one distance and make it their own. The 100 meters, for example, is a totally different event from the 400

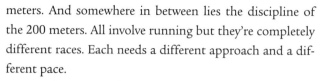

meters. And somewhere in between lies the discipline of the 200 meters. All involve running but they're completely different races. Each needs a different approach and a different pace.

It's the same with worship leading. And again, versatility is the keyword. Some of us may be able to lead in a cell-group, or home-group, setting, but how good are we at adapting ourselves to leading a congregation (lots of cells or home groups joined together)? Some of us may be called to lead in a celebration-type meeting (a worship gathering of more than one congregation), but what different approach is needed for that?

Whether we're leading worship in a cell, a congregation or a celebration, there are certain key values and principles that all have in common. Yet in another way, they're totally different "races," and each one requires a slightly different approach.

So, in which of these three settings is it the hardest to lead worship? I've thought about this for a while and have come to the conclusion that they all come out about the same. There's not really one setting in which it is harder to lead than in the others. Each group has its own advantages, but each also comes with a specific set of challenges for you to get your head around as the worship leader.

CELL

You can't beat the cell group for that intimate, raw, community vibe. If you can get it right, there's something special about singing out to God in someone's front room with little more than an acoustic guitar. It feels so uncomplicated, so free of distractions and so New Testament (apart from the acoustic guitar of course)! If we can lead people to the secret place of praise in this small setting, it can be a beautiful thing.

> WHEN WE LIFT OUR VOICES TOGETHER, WE REACH WAY BEYOND THE CONFINES OF THE ROOM AND WE TOUCH HEAVEN.

The first step is to help people realize that what we're doing goes way beyond this little room—that when we lift our voices together (however weak or thin that may sound), we reach way beyond the confines of this room and we touch heaven. Maybe we get this sense across by the way we introduce our worship, or maybe through what we pray at the beginning; however we do it, it is an essential key to unlocking a meaningful time of worship in this environment. In the down-to-earth setting of a home group, it's so important to prepare our hearts for a spiritual event. Once that happens, suddenly none of us will be focusing on what our neighbor's voice sounds like or if our own voice is in tune. We become caught up with the living God.

One of the biggest challenges of leading in this setting is that it feels so vulnerable. There is no band to hide behind, nor is there the security blanket of a microphone. It's important that we sing out confidently—this creates an environment where other people are likely to feel free to sing their hearts out, too. Sing loudly enough so that people can hear you well enough to follow along, but not so loudly that you become a distraction. Build up a vocabulary of songs— partly so that you don't have the complication of turning pages every other minute, but also so that you can flow spontaneously with a new idea at any moment. Practice tempos to songs—songs can drag very easily in this setting, in which there's no band to fill in the gaps.

Once you've got beyond some of these initial practicalities, the biggest challenge in a cell-group setting is to keep it fresh. This is a challenge when leading regularly in any worship setting, yet in a cell group it's even more acute, because you generally have fewer songs to choose from. If you take a list of all the songs you sing on a Sunday morning in the congregation, you will realize that many of these aren't appropriate or attainable when it comes to the home-group setting. Some songs have notes that are too high—you can belt them out when there's 200+ people and a rousing band to accompany the anthem; but when it comes to 5 people in your front room, with nothing but a lone acoustic guitar, things are a little more, shall we say, exposed. Other songs get ruled out because they've got male and female repeat lines. In reality, most home groups can't cope with those kinds of songs (unless the group has particularly strong and confident singers).

The most common reason why songs don't make the transition from congregation to cell is that they're too wordy. It's simply not feasible for the average person to have memorized a load of lengthy songs that they get to sing now and again on the weekend. I guess in theory you could have an overhead projector or word sheets (if you've covered the copyright aspects)—but this somehow jars with the raw, uncomplicated and intimate environment of a home group.

For me, the key is to work with sections of these songs. Maybe the chorus is instantly memorized and stands up well on its own. Or maybe you take just one easily learned verse from a hymn and segue into it at an appropriate moment when you're ending another song. You could even take just one particularly repeatable line from a song and tag it onto the end of another song, just to bring some freshness. Finally, you might want to take an up-tempo song, bring it down a few keys and use it as a slower, more tender offering. Again, this can breathe a fresh lease of life into an old song and help keep you fresh in your worship leading.

The beauty of the cell setting is that there's room to be spontaneous. The computer guy doesn't need a list of songs (because there isn't a computer guy), and you don't need to worry whether or not the band know a song (because there isn't a band). In a sense, leading worship in a cell group is like driving a little speedboat—it's easy to make various twists and turns, whether they're planned or unplanned.

CONGREGATION

When it comes to the congregation and celebration settings, you're captaining a very different ship—comparable to a big tanker ship, which takes more thought, effort and experience to make unexpected turns in.

That's not to say spontaneity is impossible in the congregation (and celebration) setting. It just has to be a little bit more rehearsed (however contradictory that sounds). In other words, you need to train your musicians (and computer operator) to be able to flow with the spontaneous. Make space in practice times to flow together spontaneously: try running songs one into the other seamlessly; try different endings; try playing songs in various keys, so you can adapt them to link with different songs. Create a team that respects the discipline of a well-rehearsed song yet is ready and able to flow with any changes of direction and approach that seem appropriate.

In reality, it's a huge step to go from leading worship in a cell group to leading in a congregational setting. The number of practical things you need to consider doubles. Anyone can play in time with themselves (well, nearly anyone!), but leading a band is a whole different thing. Practice starting and ending songs cleanly. Find some subtle hand signals (which don't resemble rude gestures!) to direct the band during unplanned moments. Make sure both you and your musicians and singers memorize as many songs as possible—so you can pay maximum attention to flowing together musically, joining with the congregation and, most of all, fixing your eyes on Jesus.

Working as part of a team is probably the biggest difference from leading alone in a small group. There are so many people to connect with and to learn to flow with:

the speaker, the band, the sound engineer, the congregation and, of course, the pastor. (Remember, the pastor is in authority—if you do not "get a witness" from your pastor on the matter, don't turn your amp up to 10!) When you arrive at church to lead worship, remember that you are coming to serve and not to be served. That will have a hugely positive bearing on your relationships with all of the above people and will ease you through a whole host of tensions that could otherwise build up.

When you lead in a cell group, it's likely that you're all of a similar age and, to some degree, the same sort of people. There's a good chance you even all like the same kinds of music. But when you come into the congregational setting, it's a whole different picture. There most probably will be lots of different age groups and types of people, with different preferred songs, styles and sounds. Again, the key is servant leadership. Find an appropriate volume for the band, one that will not alienate or offend. Don't just choose songs from your own personal preferences, but begin to find out which songs are the most helpful to various groups, in terms of leading them into worship.

As well as presenting a challenge, leading lots of different ages and types of people at one time is an amazing blessing. How many other places on Earth do you find so many different voices singing one song? If you can foster that sense of the family of God worshipping with one voice, it is an incredibly powerful thing.

CELEBRATION

Whereas the congregation feels like a great big family gathered together to worship God, the celebration setting tends to carry more the sense of a great big army. It is an amazing sense to be among many hundreds (or thousands) of worshippers gathered from a wider area.

> GREAT MUSIC ALONE CANNOT USHER IN GREAT WORSHIP—WE MUST LOOK TO THE HOLY SPIRIT'S PROMPTINGS AND BE DEPENDENT ON HIM.

Having said that, beware the allure of big things. In Kingdom terms, bigger does not necessarily mean better. For sure, a big meeting can provide a most incredible encounter with the almighty God. But if it is to be truly meaningful, we need to approach leading the meeting with a purity of heart and a focus on what we are doing.

Lesson number one for me is always this: a great band does not automatically equal great worship. In these settings there are often more musicians and singers for you to choose from, so in reality you may end up with a pretty decent band. Wonderful—as long as we don't end up losing our dependence on God. Too many times I've been tricked into thinking, *Great band, great sound system, lots of people—wow—it's going to be a great night of worship.* As soon as you catch yourself descending into this sort of thought pattern, repent and get back on track. It's essential that we stay in the place of complete dependence. Great music alone cannot usher in great worship—we must look to the Holy Spirit's promptings and be as dependent on Him as we were the very first time we ever stood up to lead.

Keep an eye on the practical things which present themselves in this situation. The band needs to be loud enough so that people can "travel together" yet not so loud that they can't hear themselves sing. Be ready to sing some songs just with voices. Don't fall into the trap of thinking you need to use the band on every single song just because it is there.

Out of the three worship settings we've looked at, this is the one where it's most likely that not everyone will know the same songs. That's definitely a big consideration. It's important to make sure that somewhere in the mix of songs are ones that every churchgoing person in the room is likely to know. Again, it's all about traveling together—it's a terrible shame if people return home having never really lifted up their many voices together as one choir.

If we can get it right in this situation, our eyes of faith will be opened up in an amazing way. Joining together like that is powerful in itself; yet deep inside we know that what we are seeing is a mere glimpse of the day when every tribe and every tongue will gather together to sing the great praises of Jesus.

Let's be versatile as lead worshippers. In every situation, learn to lead with pastoral wisdom, creative insights and sensitivity to the Holy Spirit's every whisper.

self-centered and self-consumed? The answer, bottom line, is that they have never really worshipped God. They have never bowed to Him, submitted to Him, seen Him in His glory and love, and risen up to praise Him, to make joyful noises and shouts before Him. They have

> # The psalms will teach us and reform our worship, if we will hear them.

never known this release; or if they have known it for a moment, they have refused to stay there, wedded to worship, dwelling in the presence and receiving the power of almighty God, granted to us through His Son in His Spirit.

As the end of this age draws near, the issues are increasingly clear. The battle lines are drawn. We either worship the living God, or we worship the devil with all his masks and disguises. But how shall we worship? Where will we learn to worship Him? The first answer is biblical. The psalms will teach us and reform our worship, if we will hear them. They will lead us to God-centered worship, rather than to human-centered aesthetics or theatrics. They will teach us that worship is surrender to the great King who reigns, and we will make that surrender. They will show us how to praise Him, recounting His character and His works, which make Him worthy of our praise and evoke our joy. We will also learn to wait upon Him, to sit in the silence, to listen for His voice. We will grow in the expectancy that we will hear His living word addressed to us.

> WE MUST REMEMBER HIS MIGHTY ACTS IN OUR OWN LIVES.

We will also learn to petition Him as our King and expect to receive His answers and see Him prove that He is the living God, who is active in our midst once again. We will expect to see His salvation, healing, deliverance, peace and comfort as we hear His Word and see His work. All of this will result in greater and greater surges of praise ascending to His throne, until that day when we are caught up to be with Him forever.

Psalm 150 ends the Psalter with a call to praise. The word "praise" is repeated 13 times in 6 verses. This psalm is a little introduction to and summary of what real worship is: expressing joyful delight in the presence of God.

Praise the LORD!
Praise God in His sanctuary;
Praise Him in His mighty firmament!
(v. 1, *NKJV*).

Verse 1 opens with the common exhortation, "Praise the LORD!" It addresses all of us together and answers the question of *what* we are to do when we come into the presence of the mighty King. We come offering Him our cries and shouts of glory to His name. We come expressing our love, our delight and our adoration to Him. But where are we to do this?

First, we are to praise God "in His sanctuary." This, of course, is His Temple or palace in Jerusalem. Down through the generations as long as the Temple stood, the Jews went up to Jerusalem to worship the Lord. With the coming of Jesus, however, the veil of the Temple, which separated the people from the holy presence of God, was removed; and the Temple itself was later destroyed in judgment. Now we worship God through the temple of the risen body of Jesus Himself (see John 2:13-22), and as believers, we are all incorporated into that body. Our individual bodies (in reflection of His) also have become little temples where God chooses to dwell by His Spirit (see 1 Cor. 6:19). Today, as we gather in corporate worship, we are the living temple of God, and we are the Body of Christ in ministry together.

We also worship God "in His mighty firmament!" He is to be worshipped across the vast expanse of heaven. Heaven and Earth are to join together and become one in praising Him (see Ps. 148).

Praise Him for His mighty acts;
Praise Him according to His excellent greatness!
(Ps. 150:2, *NKJV*).

What is our motive as we come into the presence of the Lord to praise Him? First, we are to "praise Him for His mighty acts." To do this we must remember the great things He has done in creation and in history. His acts reveal His character. Through them we learn of the Creator's majesty. Through them we learn of His awesome righteousness and justice as He pounds Egypt with plagues and tears down the walls of Jerusalem. And through them we learn of His love and mercy, His covenant-treaty with us and His faithfulness toward us, consummated in the New Covenant in His Son's blood.

We must also remember His mighty acts in our own lives. He provides for us day by day. He enters our lives through His Spirit. He answers our prayers. He delivers us from our enemies. He heals our diseases. He unites us to each other in love. He matures us in His Word. He employs us in His kingdom work, and He remains faithful. Indeed, "Praise Him for His mighty acts."

We are also to "praise Him according to His excellent greatness!" (literally, "the multitude of His greatness"[1]). God is great; He is full of greatness. No one is greater than He. We praise Him for who He is, not only for what He has done. He is the mighty King. He is the eternal God. He is the source of all things; all things come from Him and return to Him. He is filled with holiness, justice, trustworthiness and covenant love. He is the alpha and the omega. He is the beginning and the end. Worship this great God. Our motives for praise are twofold: We praise God for what He has done, and we praise Him for who He is. But how are we to praise His name?

Praise Him with the sound of the trumpet;
Praise Him with the lute and harp!
Praise Him with the timbrel and dance;
Praise Him with stringed instruments and flutes!
Praise Him with loud cymbals;
Praise Him with clashing cymbals!
Let everything that has breath praise the LORD.
Praise the LORD! (vv. 3-6, *NKJV*).

The psalmist offers us the means of our praise as he describes the ancient musical instruments of Israel. God is to be praised with the "sound of the trumpet" (the ram's horn, used for signaling), the "lute" (a several-stringed instrument with a sound chamber), the "harp," the "timbrel" (a woman's instrument used in dance), "stringed instruments," "flutes," "loud cymbals" and "clashing cymbals" (types of percussion instruments). God is to be praised by a symphony of sound. Today we may legitimately add our own musical instruments to the list. Everything that evokes praise or expresses praise is a legitimate instrument of praise and therefore relevant for the culture using it. The issue is not which instruments we use; instead it is why we use them and how we use them.

Our voices lifted in praise are to be accompanied by instruments of praise. We are also to "dance" (v. 4). Physical expressions in worship are important. The real issues are whether or not such dance comes from the heart, is Spirit-led (rather than for show) and is appropriate to the gathering. Ask, Is it presented as an offering to almighty God?

As this psalm and the Psalter concludes, there is another exhortation, which refers us back to verse 1: "Let everything that has breath praise the LORD." The animals have breath; they are to praise the Lord. The birds have breath; they are to praise the Lord. Humans have breath;

they are to praise the Lord. This is the purpose of breath—the spirit (*ruach*) which God breathed into us (see Gen. 2:7). We are to breathe it back to Him in praise, as we offer the essence of our lives up to Him. Indeed, as the psalm ends, "Praise the LORD!"

the one thing...

GRAHAM ORD

I often think about worship leading as pastoring people through music. Our music helps people to meet with Jesus, and in turn, we are expectant that Jesus will meet with them. In this way, worship leading takes on a pastoral role.

People are very precious. Through loving them, we are kept in touch with the fragile nature of life—and also with our desperate need for God. Compassion curbs our tendencies toward selfishness. By developing pastoral hearts, we gain the sensitivity we vitally need to lead people before the One who is *more than enough* for them. We should always stay profoundly aware that our music in itself is actually powerless to save anyone.

WHAT A BAND WANTS FROM THEIR WORSHIP LEADER

MATT WEEKS

Worship leading is mostly looked at through the lens of how the lead worshipper relates to the congregation—and rightly so. Yet there is another dynamic at play: you've got to lead your band, too. So what does a band want from you, their leader?

First, *confidence*. A band will respond much better when you exude a certain amount of confidence. Not arrogance in any respect but a humble confidence—the sense that you know where you are heading and how you will get there.

Second, *communication*. Once you have decided on a vision, or direction, you must then communicate this vision clearly to the band. Most musicians will respond to your confidence enthusiastically, but it may not necessarily be the exact way that you expected them to respond. Remember, always overcommunicate rather than undercommunicate.

Third, *encouragement*. If you've started to communicate to your players and singers, your feedback on how they are doing is extremely vital. Whether you need to communicate something again or just say it was exactly right, your encouragement to them is so important. This applies not only to their musical activity but to their spiritual activity, too.

Your role contains a combination of musical and pastoral aspects. A band will look for maturity in both areas from you, their worship leader. Musical maturity will help you understand where your band members are coming from—from their musical preferences right down to the suggestions they make during rehearsal times. It also gives your team more confidence in the decisions you make. So, aim to learn a little bit more about the theories and techniques behind what you do, while you broaden your listening vocabulary, too.

Pastoral maturity is important because musicians can be tender and fragile souls. They often make themselves vulnerable by putting their heart into expressing something which could be torn down or easily ignored. Aim to be approachable and encouraging.

It's well worth being aware of the different types of musicians and singers that may be a part of your team. In very broad terms there are two types of performers, and most members of your worship team will fit somewhere along the spectrum between these two extremes. At one end you have a less experienced and less confident player or singer, and at the other end you find the experienced, confident player or singer.

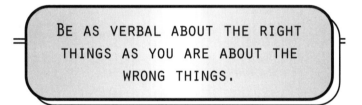

BE AS VERBAL ABOUT THE RIGHT THINGS AS YOU ARE ABOUT THE WRONG THINGS.

All musicians and singers will benefit from encouragement, whether they are beginners or seasoned performers. Whereas the less experienced and unsure musicians and singers may want you to encourage them by *taking* them under your wing, the more experienced performers are more likely to want you to encourage them in ways that *give* them wings and release them.

Whatever level a musician or singer is at, tell him or her if it's right! So often a worship leader will point out things that are wrong or that need to be altered. If musicians and singers aren't told what is good, too, they may never quite be sure if what they are playing is appropriate. Be as verbal about the right things as you are about the wrong things.

Last, *environment* is everything. Try to create an atmosphere where your musicians and singers feel safe and are free to be creative. Given space to experiment, a band will grow in skill, confidence and unity.

the one thing...

(T O M   L A N E)

What has helped me the most as a leader in worship?
Honesty. Since God already knows what's in my heart,
I obviously can't fool or impress Him, so I've learned to be
real with Him. Every time I get up to lead people, I am
totally aware of how very little I really have to offer Him in
the way of assistance.

WORSHIP AND JUSTICE

An Interview with Mike Pilavachi

What is the link between worship and justice?

There are many ways to live out our worship, and pursuing God's heart of justice for the poor and the broken is one of them. Worship and justice are two sides of the same coin, and they're inextricably linked.

A key Scripture that's challenged me is Amos 5:23-24. These verses say, "Away with the noise of your songs! I will not listen to the music of your harps. But let justice roll on like a river, righteousness like a never-failing stream!" Here you get a sense of God's anger and broken heart at a people who may have sung all the right songs and done all the right things in the Temple and, yet, whose lives were not matching up. They weren't living out God's justice. They failed to see that actually to care for the poor, the broken, the oppressed and those on the margins of society is an important aspect of worship.

So where does that leave us in terms of singing our worship songs?

We don't want to downplay the role of singing the songs or reject what we do in the gathered community. And we certainly don't want to downplay adoration. But to simply gaze into the eyes of our heavenly Father while we look with contempt on the poor, the broken and the despised is a contradiction in terms.

John says in his first letter, "If anyone says, 'I love God,' yet hates his brother, he is a liar. For anyone who does not love his brother, whom he has seen, cannot love God, whom he has not seen" (1 John 4:20). In a sense it's as simple as that. It's reconnecting what we do when we sing with the whole of our lives.

Jesus will say to the righteous, "I was hungry and you fed Me, thirsty and you gave Me a drink, naked and you clothed Me." The righteous will say, "When were You hungry and we fed You?" And Jesus will say, "When you did it to the least of these, you did it to Me" (see Matt. 25:34-40). He's explicitly saying that how we treat the poor and the outcasts of society is inextricably linked with what we offer Him. When we really live out a life

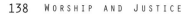

of worship, it makes what we do when we sing so much more meaningful.

Some people would argue that if we are to live lives caring for the poor, then why waste time and money in improving the quality of music or PA systems, when that money could be given to the poor? What would you say to that?

That was exactly what was said to Mary Magdalene when she broke the alabaster jar of perfume all over Jesus' feet—perfume which was worth over a year's wages. She poured it over Jesus, and it was extravagant and it was wasteful. The question was asked, "Why wasn't this perfume sold and the money given to the poor?" Jesus' response was, "You will always have the poor among you, but you will not always have Me" (see John 12:1-8).

The Lord called Israel to give of their best for the Temple and bring sacrifices to God. When we do that, there will always be more than enough left over to give to the poor. It's when we have a poverty mentality to God that somehow we find we don't have enough resources to give to the poor.

If we're not extravagant in our worship of Jesus, then we're actually nothing more than glorified social workers.

How do we work this out practically in our everyday lives?

We try to find all sorts of ways to flesh out our pursuit of worship and justice. On a Sunday we have a black plastic bin at the front of the church. Someone said once that a church's architecture reflects its theology. So if a church

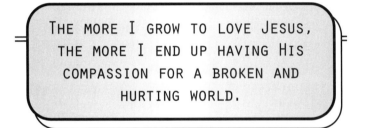

THE MORE I GROW TO LOVE JESUS, THE MORE I END UP HAVING HIS COMPASSION FOR A BROKEN AND HURTING WORLD.

has a big altar table and candles, you know that they have a certain theology. If there's a big pulpit with an eagle, made of brass, staring down, you say that they have a certain theology. Well, we have this black bin at the front of our church; and during the offering, when we tithe our money to the Lord's work, we also bring food and other items. These are given to the social services, who distribute them to people in need. It's symbolic—this big black bin reminds us as we worship that we must always remember the poor.

The most interesting thing for me, as the pastor, is that the people most active in ministering to the broken seem to be the ones most engaged in worship on a Sunday, too. It's not either-or; it's two sides of the same coin. I know for me the more I grow to love Jesus, the more I end up having His compassion for a broken and hurting world.

We must worship God with adoration, praise and thanksgiving in the temple; then from that place go out in power to live a life that's pleasing to Him.[1]

the one thing...

(N I G E L   M O R R I S)

Our worship of Jesus is always a response to who He is or, rather, how we perceive Him to be. If He is somewhat small in our hearts and minds, our response may remain minimal, mechanical and even miserly. But as we see Him more and more for who He really is, realizing what He has done for us, then pouring out our lives and resources will be our joyful response and our heart's desire.

theology of worship

UNDERSTANDING WORSHIP

(PART 3)

CHRIS JACK

Forms of Worship in the Old Testament

"Worship is not a recent invention," Derek Tidball reminds us in his brief study of worship in *On the Bridge*.[1] The roots of Christian worship reach back well over 2,000 years, to the Old Testament era. Indeed, we cannot properly understand New Testament teaching about worship without an appreciation of worship in the Old Testament.

For many Christians, the Old Testament remains a mysterious and seemingly irrelevant book. At no point does it appear more distant from the needs and aspirations of people in secularised cultures than when it focuses on the temple, the sacrificial system and the priesthood. Yet these institutions were at the very heart of ancient thinking about worship and their significance must be grasped if New Testament teaching is to be properly understood.[2]

This is why we begin with the Old Testament, despite the fact that its worship looks so different from what we are familiar with as Christians. I can't recall ever attending a Sunday service at which a bull or a lamb was offered as a

> WITHIN THE OLD TESTAMENT THERE IS CONSIDERABLE DIVERSITY IN THE FORMS USED TO EXPRESS WORSHIP.

burnt offering, yet we'll see that although Christian worship is very different in many of its particulars from Old Testament worship, patterns and values are to be found in the Old Testament which are foundational for Christian worship today.

We are talking of Old Testament worship as if it were a single, uniform entity; yet, the first thing we must note is that within the Old Testament there is considerable diversity in the forms used to express worship. The Old Testament is, of course, a sizeable body of literature. Its 39 books were written over a lengthy period of time and span at least several millennia of history. During this time, from the patriarchs to the postexilic era, worship was by no means static. It underwent change. It developed. This development is essentially due, on the one hand, to God's continuing (progressive) revelation of himself and of his requirements for His people and, on the other, to the changing circumstances and contexts in which God's people found themselves.

An example of this, focusing on the locus of worship (the place where worship regularly took place), is found in the table below.

DEVELOPMENTS IN OLD TESTAMENT WORSHIP

Patriarchal Period	*Sacred Places*
Exodus—Settlement in Canaan	*Tabernacle*
Monarchy	*Temple*
Exile	*Synagogues*
Restoration	*Second Temple*

Behind the apparently simple matter of where people worshipped stands a whole range of associated issues which reflect something of the variety and diversity of Old Testament worship practices, as we shall see.

During the patriarchal period (the time of Abraham, Isaac, Jacob and Joseph), worship was largely informal. A reading of their stories, narrated in Genesis, reveals that, often, no formal requirements for worship were set out; there were no set patterns of worship; there was no absolute requirement to offer sacrifices; there were no set rituals for offering sacrifices when such were part of the worship; there was no fixed location, either in terms of a temple or a fixed shrine; and there was no established priesthood. It is true that on occasion some directions were given (see Gen. 15:9); but these were related to a specific act of worship, rather than representing the establishing of norms. Here, sacrifice is a common, though not essential, element of worship. As an example see the story of Jacob at Bethel in Genesis 28:10-22.

Worship could be offered anywhere; it was not restricted to set locations. However, certain locations did take on particular significance by association with an encounter with God that had taken place there. Altars were erected and became sacred places especially appropriate for offering sacrifices and for further meetings with

God (see Gen. 35:1-14). Nevertheless, these sacred places never became the exclusive worship sites; there was always the possibility of a significant encounter with God at a new location that then became a new sacred place. God was not bound to any one location or group of sites.

Patriarchal worship was spontaneous, involving response to a particular revelation of God or to some intervention of His on behalf of the worshipper. It was generally an individual's response, or that of a family, so it was intensely personal.

> [Patriarchal worship] is divinely initiated and motivated. . . . The worship of God only occurs as he chooses to reveal aspects of his divine purpose and character to human beings through word and deed . . . the worship of God is a response to this divine self-disclosure.[3]

The pattern of worship which emerged during the patriarchal era in the book of Genesis, then, was one that was informal, flexible, spontaneous and personal. It was always a response to God's initiative.

Although the external form of worship underwent significant changes during the Exodus period, the worship offered was no less conditioned by God's initiative.

It was in fact a response to God's momentous act of deliverance, the Exodus. This was, for the Israelites, the greatest single initiative God (Yahweh) ever took on their behalf, perpetually commemorated in the feast of the Passover. Of course, the Passover, as well as being a time of remembrance, is also a significant act of worship.

The Exodus, God's redemptive act by which the Israelites were gloriously delivered from slavery in Egypt (see Exod. 1—15), is the defining event in Israel's history. It's an event often referred to in later times (over 120 references in the Old Testament). Through the Exodus and the subsequent encounter with God at Sinai (see Exod. 19), Israel was established as the people of God. The basis of this unique relationship is the covenant God made with His people (see Exod. 19:1-8). The terms of the covenant were set out in the Law, which God gave them there.

A further provision of God at Sinai was the cult (or cultus). This is the shorthand term used to encompass all that was involved in the formal worship centered at the Tabernacle (and later, the Temple), with its system of sacrifices, priesthood, rituals and sacred objects. In the context of the giving of the Law and the detailed instructions concerning the construction of the Tabernacle and the worship to be conducted there, a fundamental worship principle is highlighted: obedience to God.

Absolute obedience to God the Creator and Redeemer is required as the basic necessary attitude of the people who truly worship God.[4]

At Sinai, God laid down for His people the actual forms in which worship should be expressed. And central to this was sacrifice. Sacrifice played a central role in the corporate worship of Israel. Furthermore, there was just one official sanctuary where sacrifice was to be offered: the Tabernacle. For details, see Exodus 25—31; 35—40; and also the book of Leviticus.

So once again, worship was seen to be a response to God's initiative. More than that, it also became a response to His specific directives. He told His people precisely *how* they were to worship Him. This was a clear development from the much more informal worship offered in the patriarchal era.

The Tabernacle was a portable sanctuary. In time, once the Israelites were settled in the land of Canaan, the Promised Land, the Tabernacle was replaced by the Temple. The latter, built by King Solomon, was a more permanent sanctuary located in Jerusalem (see 1 Kings 5—7; 2 Chron. 2—4). Once the Temple had been completed, the Ark of the Covenant, which symbolized the very presence of God, was transferred to it; and the Temple was dedicated (see 1 Kings 8; 2 Chron. 5—7). The description of the accompanying phenomena of cloud and fire, associated in the text with the glory of God (see 2 Chron. 5:13-14; 7:1-3), has strong parallels with the account following the completion of the Tabernacle in Exodus 40:34-38. These parallels confirm the legitimacy of the Temple as the new sanctuary.

In practice, other than a tendency toward elaboration in the ceremonial associated with the rituals that were undoubtedly fostered by the sheer grandeur of the new surroundings, little changed. Temple worship was essentially a continuation of Tabernacle worship.

The cataclysmic events of the exile, with the destruction of Jerusalem and its Temple together with the deportation of many of its inhabitants, brought enforced changes to Israel's worship. With no recognized sanctuary, no cult and no focal meeting place, the Jews had to adapt. They did so by giving a central role to the Torah, the Law, as enshrined in their Scriptures. They became increasingly a people of the Book. Although the origin of the synagogues (such a prominent feature in the Gospels) is far from clear, it is widely held that it was during the exile that they came into being. These were not minitemples, for no cult was practiced there. Rather, they were meeting places where the faithful gathered to pray and to read the Torah.

Following the exile, when Jews returned to Jerusalem (the restoration), the Temple was rebuilt and the cult reinstated. This is often referred to as the Second Temple period. It continued right through until the destruction of the Temple by the Romans in A.D. 70. The restoration should not be imagined simply as a return to how things were.

> CHANGING FORMS BUT CONSISTENT HEART AND CENTER—ISRAEL'S LEGITIMATE WORSHIP WAS ALWAYS A RESPONSE TO GOD'S INITIATIVE.

While there was a return to Temple-centered worship, synagogues, especially those that were geographically removed from the Temple, continued to have their own role; and the Torah maintained its place as a controlling factor in Jewish life and religion, with the increasing dominance of those with authority to teach it (the scribes) and with an all-too-frequent drift toward legalism in interpretation and application.

The 1500 years from the days of Abraham to the time of Ezra (c. 1900-450 B.C.) saw many great changes in the form of worship in ancient Israel. . . . If the form of worship changed with times and situations, its heart and centre did not.[5]

Changing forms but consistent heart and center—Israel's legitimate worship was always, whatever its actual form, a response to God's initiative and an expression of obedience to him.

the one thing...

(A N D R E W   M A R I E S)

Balance up the corporate aspect of worship and understand that the presence of Jesus is not just found "beyond the veil" in an individual experience of personal and intimate worship but that we're really called to worship *together* as the Body of Christ. Saint Paul in Ephesians 1:23 says that the Church is "the *fullness* of Him who fills all in all" (*NKJV*, emphasis added). We're seriously losing this today and have been too influenced by the individualistic, consumerist approach of the rest of society. Let's begin to sing a lot more about *we* rather than just *I*.

WHAT A WORSHIP LEADER LOOKS FOR IN A BAND

(TIM HUGHES)

As a worship leader, it's essential to be a part of a team that gels together, is for each other and gets passionate about God together. Surround yourself with musicians and singers who are true worshippers. Being involved in a worship team is very different from being involved in a rock band. As a worship band your focus is on God and on leading His people into His presence. It is not about entertaining people with a few classic Christian hits. A worship band, by its very definition, must be made up of worshippers. This seems obvious, but in practice it can be so tempting to put the emphasis on the quality of musicianship, compromising heart standards for the sake of that long-sought-after drummer.

Next, find people who will buy into your vision and support what you're doing, both in their hearts and with their music. With these essential ingredients in place, there are several other qualities I look for in a worship band.

I always start by looking at character. The attitude of those involved is *always* more important than the gifting. First, do they walk humbly? It's so important that the

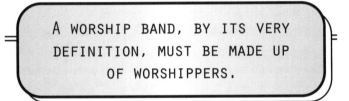

A WORSHIP BAND, BY ITS VERY DEFINITION, MUST BE MADE UP OF WORSHIPPERS.

members of the worship team aren't up in front trying to impress people or feed their insecure egos. Again, it sounds fairly obvious; yet you'd be surprised how many musicians have learned their craft in an environment where the emphasis is on impressing people. In worship, though, there is no room for performance.

If I'm thinking about using someone on the worship team, I observe them at church. Now I'm not talking about obsessively stalking them and tapping their phone—but spending time with them and looking to see if they really enter in to worship on a regular basis. Do they attend church when they're not playing? How do they treat others in your church? These are all clues to a person's character. Of course, be careful—for ultimately who are we to judge? Yet a certain level of discernment is needed when you're looking to involve new people.

Then look for a teachable heart. As part of a team you are always learning together. There are some very joyful times, but there are also some difficult things to face. Sometimes as a worship leader you may have to challenge some of your band members on attitude issues. There is a great team-building dynamic when you are able to challenge someone and they take it on board humbly, instead of grudgingly or defensively. A friend of mine who leads worship once mentioned to a fairly experienced guitarist that he felt this guitarist needed to be more creative in his playing. This guitarist quickly took the advice and again invested in lessons to improve his creativity. What a great example of a teachable spirit.

Next, examine their attitude toward others. Being involved in worship will inevitably mean being involved with a church, and to some degree we're all called to be pastors to the people we're leading. Every musician must work on his or her pastoral awareness. I love it when I see the musicians involve themselves with the people at the meetings. To me this models something very important. It demonstrates that everyone is working together and that just because someone is on a stage, it doesn't make him or her any more important.

Once you've looked at character, move on to musicality. Though not ultimately *the* most important factor in what worship leaders want from their band, it is a pretty important one. Someone may have the heart and the values, but if they can't play an instrument or sing in tune, maybe their calling isn't to be playing or singing on the worship team. At times I've played with people whose standard of play actually distracted people's attention away from God and instead onto their hideously out-of-tune guitar or total lack of rhythm on the drums!

Look for creativity. I always love to be stretched creatively. Leading worship regularly, it's easy to become stale at times, so to have team members who keep challenging you to stay fresh musically is brilliant. Some musicians are brilliant at coming up with different sounds and ideas; having them in the band can really stretch you as the worship leader.

I once heard someone say that if you have five members in a band, everyone should play one-fifth of the overall music. The implication is that every band member needs to be a team player. It can be frustrating when musicians disappear into their own little world, totally unaware of what everyone else is playing. One sign of a team player is sensitivity to noise levels on stage. Everyone must keep his or her instrument at a level that serves the congregation and prefers the other members of the worship team.

At the end of the day, this is what you're looking for in a band: servants—people who will serve the church and support your leadership, as together you worship God.

the one thing...

DAPHNE RADEMAKER

Let God be your defense and your advertiser. I continue to learn over and over that we don't need to make room for ourselves or strive to become a part of things. We just need to work on our craft and knock on God's door with what we have to offer.

We can give even when we are taken advantage of—and then go right back in and give again. There's a distinct difference between trying to gain favor with people and doing what God's asked you to do. Let's always do it God's way.

WORSHIP WITH ALL YOU HAVE!

Don Williams

Reflections on Psalm 100

A psalm. For giving thanks.

Shout for joy to the LORD, all the earth.
>   Worship the LORD with gladness;
>   come before him with joyful songs.
Know that the LORD is God.
>   It is he who made us, and we are his;
>   we are his people, the sheep of his pasture.
Enter his gates with thanksgiving
>   and his courts with praise;
>   give thanks to him and praise his name.

For the LORD is good and his love endures forever;
 his faithfulness continues through all generations.

Worship with all you have!

Worship is an event. We don't simply come to worship
or attend worship; we do worship. This summons to worship is a summons to action: "shout" (a shout of triumph
or a battle cry), "worship" (literally, "serve," like a slave),
"come," "enter," "give thanks" and "praise." When we do
this, we throw ourselves into it. It's hard to shout without
using our whole body. We open our mouth. We fill our
lungs. We let go. When we enter Yahweh's gates with
thanksgiving and His courts with praise, we are in motion.
We are going somewhere—into the Temple to see the King.
This worship, or service, is corporate, intense, loud, boister-
ous, energetic, releasing. It is worthy of our great God.

This worship also has a tone. We shout "for joy." We worship "with gladness." We come "with joyful songs." We enter
"with thanksgiving and . . . praise." We "give thanks to him"
and we "praise his name." Do you feel this? Exhilaration,
gladness, exuberance, even ecstasy? Can you see faces with
eyes wide open, expansive looks, brows raised, mouths smil-
ing and laughing—all also sweat-stained on a hot Jerusalem
day? It is holy hilarity, worthy of Majesty.

Psalm 100 is antiphonal. The worship leaders and the worshippers dialogue. This worship is active, reactive and dynamic. Unlike many people attending our churches, there are no passive observers here.

The priests at the Temple gates summon the pilgrims: "Shout for joy to the LORD, all the earth. Worship the

THE ACTION OF WORSHIP, THE *HOW*, IS BASED UPON REVELATION, THE *WHY*.

LORD with gladness; come before him with joyful songs." The crowds respond with their confession: "Know that the LORD is God. It is he who made us, and we are his; we are his people, the sheep of his pasture." Again, the priests call: "Enter his gates with thanksgiving and his courts with praise; give thanks to him and praise his name." The people respond: "For the Lord is good and his love endures forever; his faithfulness continues through all generations."

Notice that the action of worship, the *how*, is based upon revelation, the *why*. We—and the whole earth—worship with such delight (vv. 1-2) because Yahweh ("the LORD") is God (implying that all other gods are not gods;

v. 3). He is our Creator: "It is he who made us." We are neither self-sufficient nor autonomous. He is our Owner:
"We are his." But he is also our Redeemer calling us to be
His covenant nation: "We are his people, the sheep of his
pasture." (Kings in the ancient world were often symbolized as shepherds; see Psalm 23.)

Again, the how, our entering the Temple, giving
thanks to Him and praising His name (v. 4), is because of
the why: "For the LORD [Yahweh] is good [steadfast in his
moral character and justice] and his [covenant] love
endures forever; his faithfulness [trustworthiness] continues through all generations" (v. 5).

Does our worship measure up to these biblical tests?
When we lead worship, do we expect things to happen? Are
we participating in an event? Are we interacting with the
worshippers we lead; is our worship dialogical? Does joy
expressed by rejoicing in song mark our entrance into God's
presence? Are we taking our people there? Is this joy mere
emotion or is it grounded in our Creator, our covenant
King—with His attributes of goodness, eternal love and
faithfulness through all generations?

Don't hold back. Worship costs us everything and we
are made for exactly that. Our ancestors knew this: "Man's
chief end is to glorify God, and to enjoy him forever."[1] Do
we?

the one thing...

PAUL OAKLEY

Sometimes simple ideas are the best. The biggest challenge is to find fresh ways to express ancient truths that have already been written about for hundreds of years and to find fresh ways to respond to and apply those things.

songwriting

CONTENT VERSUS ENGAGEMENT

MATT REDMAN

When it comes to writing congregational song lyrics, it seems to me that two extremes often occur. Some worship songs take the heavy-on-content route—packed full of biblical phrases and meaty theology. It's the kind of song that needs chewing on. Other songs take the opposite approach—simple, uncomplicated love songs with a big emphasis placed on engaging with God.

There's definitely room for both types of songs in our worship; yet, as with so many things, it can be a little unhealthy if either of the two approaches is taken to an extreme. On one end of the spectrum, you can write a song that is so wordy and crammed full of intricate theology and deep truth, that singing it, unfortunately, becomes simply an intellectual exercise, rather than an outpouring of the heart. At the other extreme, it's also possible to write a worship song so raw and touchy-feely in its approach that it captures no real sense of who God is, and therefore it seems shallow.

The key is to find a good balance between the content and engagement factors. I once heard someone comment on the well-known "worship in spirit and truth" passage from John 4. This person reflected that our worship songs need to have a sense of being a spiritual event, yet they also need to be clothed richly in the truth of who God is and what He has done. Some of the most valuable worship songs illuminate lyrically the beautiful truths of God yet also give us space to reflect, respond and engage with Him.

Recently I came across a Scripture that I thought really suited this ideal. Over the last few months I've had my heart set on writing some simpler songs, and for me this portion of the Bible said it all. Ecclesiastes 5:2 tells us: "God is in heaven, and you are on the earth, so let your words be few." In verse 7 it urges us: "Therefore, stand in awe of God."

In this chapter of the Bible, in just over 20 words, is a fantastic song-birthing piece of truth. Of course, there's a time to excitedly express to God everything that's on our hearts—the overflow of love and wonder. Yet there's also time to quiet down and simply stand in awe of Him with the simplest of songs and the fewest of words.

So how do we pursue a healthy balance of content and engagement in our quest to write God-honoring, church-friendly worship songs? First of all, make sure the song starts off as worship. It seems obvious to say, but if a song is written to end up in worship, it must be birthed in worship. Maybe the Holy Spirit has been highlighting a particular theme in your church, a theme that has begun to

> IF A SONG IS WRITTEN TO END UP IN WORSHIP, IT MUST BE BIRTHED IN WORSHIP.

burn in your own heart. Find space to respond to God around that theme and worship Him. A song that starts off as little more than a cerebral exercise will probably end up being no more than that in a congregation. But a song that begins its life as a passionate time of engaging with God will hopefully carry that same dynamic with it into a congregational setting.

Then comes the perspiration. Once the initial inspiration has been poured out, most songs need to be crafted and worked on before they are suitable for congregational use. Spend time being ruthless with your lyrics. There are always lots more options available to you than you may realize at first. Take the theme of the song and study it. There are many ways to do this. One easy way is to find a concordance and simply look up the song's theme to see if any other Scriptures are suitable for your lyrics. It's a great way to have a Bible study. You might also refer to some old hymns and see if they inspire you with fresh ideas as you pursue the theme of your song.

One thing to keep in mind is that simple doesn't have to mean shallow. I've been challenging myself to write songs which are short enough to be memorized quickly yet have some sort of depth to the lyrics, in terms of the revelation of Jesus. Let's aim to write songs that reveal something of the wonderful mysteries of God and at the same time give the worshipper space to respond to Him simply and wholeheartedly.

the one thing...

ANDY PIERCY

Spend time learning the craft of songwriting. Not many people write their best songs straight away.

Your songwriting will benefit enormously from the time and effort being given to it. Just because the best songwriters make it appear easy, don't be fooled into thinking that it is. Remember the "10 percent inspiration and 90 percent perspiration" rule. Even inspired songs usually benefit from a refining process.

And don't feel you have to make every song idea work. Always remember that the widely sung songs are the cream of the crop. Even your favorite writers come up with stuff that simply gets thrown away.

UNDERSTANDING WORSHIP

(PART 4)

CHRIS JACK

The Heart of Worship in the Old Testament

Contrary to a popular misconception, worship in the Old Testament is more than its external form. Although at times great attention is given to the rituals involved, mere ritual is never acceptable on its own, however outwardly correct it might be. There is, in fact, throughout the Old Testament, a constant emphasis on the worshipper's having the right attitude of heart toward God if his or her worship is to be acceptable.

Having a right heart before God, or personal piety, is
a prerequisite for all true worship.

> Personal piety then is the one necessary precondi-
> tion for all Hebrew worship, the formal and the
> informal, the spontaneous and the structured,
> the individual and the corporate.[1]

The Old Testament has a great deal to say about *false
worship*. False worship involves one of three things:

1. Worshipping the wrong thing=Idolatry
2. Worshipping with the wrong heart (attitude)=
   Formalism
3. Worship divorced from an appropriate lifestyle=
   Hypocrisy

Idolatry was rampant in the nations surrounding Israel. In
essence, idolatry is the worship of anyone or anything but
the one true God. In practice, idolatry frequently involved
the worship of false gods, usually in the form of images of
some kind. It was also often bound up with immoral practices such as ritual prostitution, child sacrifice, etc.
Tragically, idolatrous worship frequently found its way into
Israelite worship. Sometimes this was in a full-blown way,
but more commonly it involved some form of syncretism—

in other words, elements of legitimate worship were preserved and blended with extraneous and illegitimate elements from Canaanite and other systems.

Worship of anything other than the one true God is prohibited by the first commandment (see Exod. 20:3), while the worship of an image of any kind is forbidden by the second (see Exod. 20:4-6). Further denunciations of idols and idolatry abound in the Old Testament (see Lev. 26:1; Deut. 27:15; 1 Sam. 15:23; 1 Kings 14:9; Ps. 78:58; Isa. 42:17; Jer. 7:30; Ezek. 14:4; 23:49). Idolatry is also expressly repudiated in the New Testament (see 1 Cor. 10:14; Gal. 5:20; Col. 3:5; 1 Pet. 4:3).

> **PRAISE IS TO BE OFFERED NOT MERELY WITH THE LIPS BUT WITH ONE'S WHOLE BEING.**

So far so good. Worshipping other gods, deflecting worship from the one true God, is clearly unacceptable. An equally unacceptable approach to worship, however, is that which preserves the externals but reduces reality to ritual. Mere *formalism*—going through the motions, performing the correct rituals but without the corresponding right attitude of heart—is condemned as vigorously as idolatry (see Pss. 24:3-6; 51:6,9,16-17; Isa. 66:1-4). Conversely, praise is to be offered not merely with the lips but with one's whole being (see Pss. 103:1; 119:7; Isa. 29:13; Jer. 12:2).

A further type of false worship is that which is not accompanied by a corresponding life of obedience to God's commands. Failing to live in a way that is consistent with being in relationship with God while outwardly offering worship to Him is pure *hypocrisy*. This is also roundly condemned (see 1 Sam. 15:22; Jer. 7:21-24; Amos 5:7-12,21-24; see also Pss. 40:6-10; 50:13-15). These passages are very sobering and are worth taking time to read and reflect on. At first sight it seems strange that at times God should appear to despise or reject the very sacrificial system he had given. However, the truth is that it is not the cult itself that God is speaking against but its abuse. Quite simply, doing the right thing with the wrong motives is just not good enough.

The heart of worship is heart-worship. And we are still in the Old Testament! What a message and challenge there is for us at a time when *how* we worship has become such a dominant, and problem, issue. The Old Testament reminds us in very clear terms that acceptable worship is always more about the attitude than the approach. The Israelites seemed to get it wrong so often. Perhaps we need to ask ourselves whether we really do any better.

So what is the heart of worship in the Old Testament? A number of key principles stand out.

1. Worship is *relational*; it involves engagement with a personal God.
2. Worship is *required* of all humanity by creation and of God's people by calling.
3. Worship is a *response* to God's initiatives in both revelation and redemption.
4. Worship involves *submission, service* and *reverence*.
5. Worship has both *individual* and *corporate* expressions.
6. Worship may be *informal* as well as *formal*.
7. Worship *changes in form* yet *is constant in its essence*.
8. Worship is about *attitude*, not just *activity*.
9. Worship is *holistic*; it involves the whole person.
10. Worship is *lifestyle* as well as *liturgy*.

There is one point that is perhaps worth underlining here: a strong emphasis on obedience runs through the Old Testament. As noted above, worship is a response to God's initiatives. And this response, if it is to be acceptable, must always be on his terms. It is true that in the time of the patriarchs, the formal requirements for worship were much less detailed and stringent than in later periods. Yet even for Abraham and the other patriarchs, God's instructions were to be obeyed when given (see Gen. 15; 17). The theme of obedience is central to the message of the book of Deuteronomy, both in relation to the keeping of the Law and in the context of offering to God acceptable worship.

Many passages could be cited here. However, one tragic story from the life of Saul highlights perhaps better than any other the seriousness of this issue. It is to be found in 1 Samuel 15. The chapter is worth reading. It is tragic-comical in the way it is recounted and is in its own right a superb example of Hebrew storytelling. The core of the story is that Saul seeks to justify not carrying out God's instructions to destroy the Amalekites totally (including livestock) by protesting that he has saved the best in order to offer it in sacrifice to God (see vv. 20-21). The response of Samuel, the prophet sent by God to confront Saul, is stinging:

> Does the LORD delight in burnt offerings and sacrifices as much as in obeying the voice of the LORD? To obey is better than sacrifice, and to heed is better than the fat of rams. For rebellion is like the sin of divination, and arrogance like the evil of idolatry. Because you have rejected the word of the LORD, he has rejected you as king (vv. 22-23).

Worship is to be offered to God on His terms, in accordance with His instructions, in the context of a life submitted to Him and obedient to His revealed will and ways. Nothing else is acceptable.

Obedience to God in cultic observance was to go hand in hand with obedience in matters of everyday life.[2]

The people of the Old Testament simply could not do it their way. Of course, neither can we.

the one thing...

RICK CUA

The thing that has motivated me most over the years is a call to excellence—not someone else's version of excellence, but my own. No matter what your skill level is, according to traditional standards, there is something special about operating at the top of your gifting. Nothing can be more distracting than the realization that someone is just getting by because of a lack of passion.

You can have the best gear, the best songs to play and a special moment to lead worship; but without the development of your skill from the inside out, you risk missing the fullness that God has ordained for that moment.

CULTIVATING A
QUIET HEART

MATT REDMAN

The '60s (so I hear) was a pretty crazy time for music. At the height of all this madness, the Beatles were huge, playing to crowds of tens of thousands. Unfortunately, back then, some of the sound equipment couldn't quite compete with the thousands of screaming fans, and the Beatles soon decided to give up playing live. As Paul McCartney explained, "We were getting worse and worse as a band while all those people were screaming. . . . It was lovely that they liked us, but we couldn't hear to play."[1]

Most of us don't have to put up with crowds of people screaming, but there are plenty of other distractions that come into play for someone involved in leading worship. So my question to myself recently has been, *Can I still hear to play?* In other words, *Am I finding enough space and peace in my life to hear the voice of the Lord prompting me and the song of the Lord inspiring me?* As lead worshippers, it's essential that we find space to breathe, time to think and moments to listen to the still small voice.

In Psalm 131 the writer declares, "I have . . . quieted my soul" (v. 2). Eugene Peterson's *THE MESSAGE* rephrases it, "I have cultivated a quiet heart." Ultimately, that is what we're talking about here. In our lives there are so many different noises that can drown out the whispers of God. As I heard Bill Hybels (Willow Creek Community Church, Chicago, Illinois) once ask, "Is the ambient noise level of my life low enough for me to hear the whispers of the Lord?" That's a great question.

Richard Swenson, in his book *Margin*, talks about the pain of overload and lists a few specific areas where our lives are getting a little too noisy. Here are a couple:

1. Activity overload—Often we end up being so busy that we try and do two or three things at once. (Ever seen someone driving their car while talking on the phone, eating a sandwich and reading a magazine?)

2. Choice overload—In 1978 there were 11,767

items in the average American supermarket. By 1992 that number had risen to 24,531 (including 186 different types of breakfast cereal found in one store).[2]

Josef Pieper, in his book *Only the Lover Sings*, puts it like this:

> Man's ability to see is in decline. Searching for the reasons we could point to several things: modern man's restlessness and stress . . . or his total enslavement by practical goals and purposes. Yet one reason must not be overlooked either: the average person of our time loses the ability to see because there is too much to see.[3]

I know this is true for me. Too often I've found myself rushing around like crazy and then filling up my precious few rest times with flicking through meaningless TV programs. Of course, we all have responsibilities in life and it's great to have some leisure time to bring a balance; but if I'm consistently finding that there's no space to listen out for the song of the Lord, then something might have to change. Creativity and the prophetic are so often birthed in the place of stillness. So often when I'm struggling to bring something fresh to the congregation, it's because I've not had time refreshing my soul before God.

> # CREATIVITY AND THE PROPHETIC ARE OFTEN BIRTHED IN THE PLACE OF STILLNESS.

Andrew Murray, in the book *Waiting on God*, looks at a couple of verses on this whole theme of stillness. Lamentations 3:26 tells us, "It is good to wait quietly for the salvation of the LORD." In Isaiah 30:15 we hear, "In quietness and trust is your strength." Murray says of these two Scriptures, "Such words reveal to us the close connection between quietness and faith. And show us what a deep need there is of quietness as an element of waiting on God."[4]

Let's be a people who seek to cultivate a quiet heart, listening constantly for the inspiring whispers of the Lord. So often, He is in the still small voice.

the one thing...

NOEL RICHARDS

Ask God to birth a big vision in your heart for the things
He wants you to do. Allow Him to fire your imagination
and put dreams within you for the sake of the Kingdom.
God is looking for a generation of musicians, singers,
dancers, writers, poets and prophets who will touch the
nations with the sounds of heaven.

RENEWING THE INTIMATE FRIENDSHIP

MATT REDMAN

With worship leading it's not *what* you know but *who* you know. I've been reminded of that recently. After a busy few months I found myself a victim once again of the Martha syndrome: so busy with the preparations and serving that I'd somehow neglected the better thing—sitting at the feet of Jesus and listening devotedly as Mary did (see Luke 10:38-42).

Don't get me wrong; I still knew how to raise my hands in the air, and I could still remember the words, chords and melodies of the songs. But it's so easy for these meaningful expressions of worship to become empty, out-ward habits. It's not *what* you know—any knowledge or experience of worship or worship leading that may have been gained means nothing at such a time. It's *who* you know—I want every word and every note to be an expression of relationship with God.

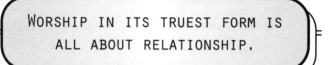

> # WORSHIP IN ITS TRUEST FORM IS ALL ABOUT RELATIONSHIP.

Worship in its truest form is all about relationship. In the *Westminster Shorter Catechism*, the chief end of man is "to glorify God, and to enjoy Him forever."[1] "To *glorify*" means to respond to this wonderful God with our lives, our deeds, our thoughts, our words and our songs. And at the same time, we should *enjoy* Him. As John Piper reminds us, "God is most glorified in us when we are most satisfied in Him."[2]

The Lord has called us to an intimate relationship with Himself. It would be an honor to merely stand from afar and revere the King of kings with our songs of praise, yet He has also called us to something deeper: a friendship with Him. This is the King of Revelation chapter 1, who majestically holds the seven stars in His right hand (see v. 16). He is the same King who in the very next verse draws near to the writer, John, and touches him with the same right hand, comforting Him and saying, "Do not be afraid" (v. 17). And the more we revere Jesus as this awesome King, the more we realize the wonder of the hand of friendship He extends to us.

Now and again we find ourselves in a place where we've lost our focus. Maybe we've been giving too much output without enough input. Maybe we're so busy that we've become distracted. I've met so many musicians in that place, and I've been there myself. God calls us back to the place of friendship.

In John 15:15, Jesus tells His disciples, "I no longer call you servants. . . . Instead, I have called you friends." Of course we're all meant to serve Him, but God is calling us deeper—to the place of friendship, a place where a mere servant could never go. Make sure, as a lead worshipper, you've not just settled for the role of servant, when a friendship with almighty God is on offer.

It's time to renew the intimate friendship. Do what you must as soon as you can, for in the end, worship leading is never really about *what* you know—it's all about *who* you know.

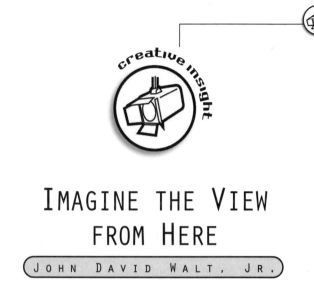

IMAGINE THE VIEW
FROM HERE

JOHN DAVID WALT, JR.

The Vision of a Lead Worshipper

Leading worship is about seeing God. The life of a worshipper, and particularly the life of a lead worshipper, is far more about a quality of vision than it is a type of personality or set of gifts. Before you can worship God, you must first see God. Worship and leading worship are about seeing God. The great worshippers of all time, the history makers, saw the Lord. They had a vision of God. "The word of the LORD came to Abram in a vision" (Gen. 15:1). Glimpsing God's glory, even from behind, empowered Moses to go forward leading the Israelites in worship. Listen to Isaiah:

"In the year that King Uzziah died, I saw the LORD seated on a throne, high and exalted, and the train of his robe filled the temple" (6:1). From Judges to Kings through the prophets and onward to the apostles, what separates their lives and work from the rest, which is to say what distinguishes their worship, is a quality of vision. They saw God and could never return to the ordinary again. Compelled by the vision of God, others followed.

Down through the centuries, the saints are set apart by their vision of God. Hear Bernard of Clairvaux on worship: "Jesus, the very thought of Thee with sweetness fills the breast; but sweeter far Thy face to see, and in Thy presence rest."[1] Thomas Aquinas, easily the greatest theologian of the medieval era, gave his life to the pursuit of the knowledge of God. The staggering influence of his scholarship is breathtaking. On December 6, 1273, while attending mass, Thomas had a vision of God. Upon being asked to write about it he responded, "Such things have been revealed to me that all that I have written seems to me as so much straw. Now I await the end of my life."[2] He never wrote again. In 1393, Julian of Norwich completed *Revelations of Divine Love*, a written account of her 16 visions of Jesus. The list goes on.

Leading worship is about seeing God. The worship songs throughout the centuries reflect this quest to see God. With a hymn we sing, "Be Thou my vision"; with a chorus, "Open our eyes, Lord, we want to see Jesus"; and with a modern worship song, "Open the eyes of my heart, Lord . . . I want to see You . . . high and lifted up, shining in the light of your glory."[3] But what is this about? In the days of the Old Testament, the question was always how one could see God and live. Today the question may be how one can see God and stay out of the psychiatric ward. So what does it mean to see God, and more so, how does it happen in a way that leads to an abandoned life of worship?

There is no formula. This is not a practical essay. Worship is not practical. Contemporary theologian Marva Dawn calls worship a royal waste of time. Worshipping God and leading others to worship Him come from the capacity of a holy imagination. This idea is not new or original, but it could be revolutionary: Worship is born from an imagination, rooted in remembrance, cultivated through attention and nurtured by discipline.

The great preachers and poets and prophets, the great songwriters and singers, are those who lived imaginatively from a vision of God. Because they saw, their leadership transformed people's ears into eyes. Hearing gives way to seeing and worship combusts into vision. Imagine. Isn't this what a lead worshipper does? It's not about singing songs but seeing God and calling others into the vision. The lead worshipper stands—no, kneels—at all the places of the wonder of God and says simply and creatively, "Imagine the view from here." The lead worshipper journeys through the stunning story of God, stopping at all the scenic overlooks and gazing on the revealed horizon of God's glory, and says clearly and profoundly, "Imagine the view from here":

Begin at the utter ends of the cosmos . . .
Immortal, invisible, God only wise, in light inaccessible hid from our eyes.[4]

Imagine the view from here.

Into the wonder of creation . . .
You spread out your arms over empty space, said let there be light in a dark and formless place the world was born. . . . What a wonderful Maker.
Shout to the Lord all the Earth let us sing, power and majesty praise to the King. Mountains bow down and the seas will roar, at the sound of your Name.[5]

Imagine the view from here.

Through the pain of rebellion and exile . . .
We bow our hearts we bend our knees, O Spirit come make us humble. We turn our eyes from evil

things, O Lord we cast down our idols. Give us clean hands and give us pure hearts, let us not lift our soul to another.[6]

Imagine the view from here.

To the place of mercy . . .
When I survey the wondrous cross on which the Prince of Glory died.
I'm forgiven because you were forsaken. I'm accepted, You were condemned.
Open up the skies of mercy, rain down the cleansing flood.
It's your kindness, Lord, that leads us to repentance. . . . It's your beauty, Lord, that makes us stand in silence. . . . Your love is better than life.[7]

Imagine the view from here.

Onward in the pilgrimage to the house of God . . .
Now you are exalted to the highest place, King of the Heavens where one day I'll bow.
How lovely is your dwelling place, O Lord Almighty. My soul longs and even faints for you.
For here my heart is satisfied within your

presence. I sing beneath the shadow of your wings. . . .
Better is one day in your courts than a thousand
elsewhere.[8]

Imagine the view from here.

And outward as apostles to the whole world . . .
Open up the doors, let the music play, let the
streets resound with singing. Songs that bring
your hope, songs that bring your joy, dancers who
dance upon injustice.[9]

Imagine the view from here.

Taking with us as many as will come upward to the place
where the streets have no name . . .
We fall down, we lay our crowns at the feet of
Jesus . . . and we cry holy, holy, holy is the Lamb.
Surrounded by your glory, what will my heart
feel? Will I dance for you Jesus or in awe of you be
still? Will I stand in your presence or to my knees
will I fall? Will I sing Hallelujah? Will I be able to
speak at all? I can only imagine.[10]

Imagine the view from here.

ENDNOTES

Revelation and Response

1. Carl "Chip" Stam, comp., "Worship Quote for the Week of January 7, 1997," *Worship Quote*, January 7, 1997. http://www.praise.net/worship/quote/q97-01-07.html (accessed December 20, 2002).

We Become Like What We Worship

1. Gerald G. May, *Addiction and Grace* (San Francisco: HarperSanFrancisco, 1988), p. 4.
2. John Bradshaw, *Bradshaw on the Family* (Deerfield Beach, FL: Health Communications, 1988), p. 20.
3. Tom Wright, *Bringing the Church to the World* (Minneapolis, MN: Bethany House Publishers, 1992), pp. 44-51.

Understanding Worship (Part 1)

1. Constance Cherry, "Worship Discipleship," *Creator*, August 30, 2002. http://www.creatormagazine.com/articles/default.asp?arttopicid=88&topicid=32&selid=1&level=3 (accessed December 18, 2002).
2. "The Shorter Catechism," in *The Book of Confessions*, part 1 of *The Constitution of the Presbyterian Church (U.S.A.)* (New York: General Assembly of the Presbyterian Church [U.S.A.], 1983), p. 7.001-.010.

Reflections on Psalm 8 (Part 2)

1. Andrew Murray, *Humility* (Pittsburgh, PA: Whitaker House, 1982), n.p.

The Cross

1. Martin Kahler, *The So-Called Historical Jesus and the Historic Biblical Christ* (Philadelphia, PA: Fortress Press, 1964), p. 80, n. 11, quoted in John T. Carrol and Joel B. Green, *The Death of Jesus in Early Christianity* (Peabody, MA: Hendrickson Publishers, 1995), p. 55.

2. Leon Morris, *The Apostolic Preaching of the Cross* (Grand Rapids, MI: Eerdmans, 1956), p. 49.

3. Ibid., p. 98.

4. Ibid., p. 114.

5. Ibid., p. 159.

6. Ibid., p. 196.

7. Ibid., pp. 248, 258.

8. N. T. Wright, *Jesus and the Victory of God* (Minneapolis, MN: Fortress Press, 1996), pp. 154-155.

9. Source unknown.

10. This verse and the previous one are two verses from "When I Survey the Wondrous Cross," by Isaac Watts (1674-1748).

11. P. T. Forsyth, *The Work of Christ* (London: 1948), p. 105, quoted in Leon Morris, *The Apostolic Preaching of the Cross* (Grand Rapids, MI: Eerdmans, 1956), p. 220.

12. James Denney, *The Death of Christ* (1902; reprint, New Canaan, CT: Keats Publishing Co., 1981), pp. 177-178.

The Real Worship Leader

1. Oswald Chambers, *My Utmost for His Highest* (Uhrichsville, OH: Barbour and Co., 1987), n.p.

Skill and Sensitivity

1. Source unknown.

2. Source unknown.

Understanding Worship (Part 2)

1. David Peterson, *Engaging with God* (Leicester, England: Apollos, 1992), p. 17.

2. Ibid., p. 56.

3. H. Schönweiss and C. Brown, "Prayer," *New International Dictionary of New Testament Theology*, vol. 2, ed. C. Brown (Exeter, England: Paternoster, 1976).

4. Andrew Hill, *Enter His Courts with Praise* (Eastbourne, England: Kingsway, 1998), p. 4.

5. A.W. Tozer, *Whatever Happened to Worship?* ed. G. B. Smith (Carlisle, England: OM Publishing, 1997), p. 57.

Praise the Lord!

1. Donald M. Williams, *The Communicator's Commentary Series, Old Testament, vol. 14: Psalms 73-150* (Dallas: Word Books, 1989), p. 541.

Worship and Justice

1. Mike Pilavachi, interview by Matt Redman, 2001.

Understanding Worship (Part 3)

1. Derek Tidball, *On the Bridge: A Study Guide for Preachers and Worship Leaders* (London, England: Baptist Union Publications, 1992), p. 17.

2. David Peterson, *Engaging with God* (Leicester, England: Apollos, 1992), p. 23.

3. Andrew Hill, *Enter His Courts with Praise* (Eastbourne, England: Kingsway, 1998), pp. 31-32.

4. Yoshiaki Hattori, "Theology of Worship in the Old Testament," in *Worship: Adoration and Action*, ed. D. A. Carson (Grand Rapids, MI: Baker, 1993), p. 28.

5. G. J. Wenham, "Worship," *Marshall Pickering Encylcopedia of the Bible*, vol. 2, ed. W. A. Elwell (London, England: Marshall-Pickering, 1990), p. 2164.

Worship with All You Have!

1. "The Shorter Catechism," in *The Book of Confessions*, part 1 of *The Constitution of the Presbyterian Church (U.S.A.)* (New York: General Assembly of the Presbyterian Church [U.S.A.], 1983), p. 7.001-.010.

Understanding Worship (Part 4)

1. Andrew Hill, *Enter His Courts with Praise* (Eastbourne, England: Kingsway, 1998), p. 11.

2. David Peterson, *Engaging with God* (Leicester, England: Apollos, 1992), p. 49.

Cultivating a Quiet Heart

1. Source unknown.

2. Richard A. Swenson, *Margin* (Colorado Springs, CO: NavPress, 1995), n.p.

3. Josef Pieper and Lothar Krauth, trans., *Only the Lover Sings* (San Francisco: Ignatius Press, 1990), n.p.

4. Andrew Murray, *Waiting on God* (Fort Washington, PA: Christian Literature Crusade, 1992), n.p.

Renewing the Intimate Friendship

1. "The Shorter Catechism," in *The Book of Confessions*, part 1 of *The Constitution of the Presbyterian Church (U.S.A.)* (New York: General Assembly of the Presbyterian Church [U.S.A.], 1983), p. 7.001-.010.

2. John Piper, *desiringGOD.org*, December 30, 2002. http://www.desiringgod.org/ (accessed December 30, 2002).

Imagine the View from Here

1. Bernard of Clairvaux, "Jesu dulcis memoria," trans. Edward Caswall, "Jesus, the Very Thought of Thee."

2. Source unknown.

3. These lyrics come from the following songs: Mary E. Byrne, trans., "Be Thou My Vision"; Robert Cull, "Open Our Eyes, Lord"; Paul Baloche, "Open the Eyes of My Heart."

4. Walter Chalmers Smith, "Immortal, Invisible, God Only Wise."

5. These lyrics come from the following songs: Matt Redman, "Wonderful Maker"; Darlene Zschech, "Shout to the Lord."

6. Charlie Hall, "Give Us Clean Hands."

7. These lyrics come from the following songs: Isaac Watts, "When I Survey the Wondrous Cross"; Billy Foote, "You Are My King"; Chris Tomlin, Jesse Reeves and Louie Giglio, "Kindness."

8. These lyrics come from the following songs: Matt Redman, "Once Again"; Matt Redman, "Better Is One Day."

9. Martin Smith, "Did You Feel the Mountains Tremble."

10. These lyrics come from the following songs: Chris Tomlin, "We Fall Down"; Bart Millard, "I Can Only Imagine."

CONTRIBUTORS

Brenton Brown is the writer of "Lord, Reign in Me" and "Your Love Is Amazing," among other Vineyard songs. Living in Oxford, England, where he heads up a worship team, he also travels widely teaching on and leading worship.

Dave Clifton is based at Holy Trinity Brompton Anglican Church in London and has written many worship songs including "Praise God from Whom All Blessings Flow," cowritten with Andy Piercy. Dave also has a great deal of experience as musical director with various artists and bands.

Rick Cua, though still active as a bass player and songwriter, currently serves as vice president, creative, at EMI Christian Music Publishing. Married to his high school sweetheart, Diana, for 31 years, Rick lives in Brentwood, Tennessee, with Diana and their two daughters, Niki and Nina.

Brian Doerksen lives in Abbotsford, British Columbia, Canada, with his wife, Joyce, and their six children. The writer of songs such as "Come, Now Is the Time," "Faithful One" and "Refiner's Fire," he regularly encourages others in the craft of composing congregational worship songs.

Wayne Drain is married to June and has three children. He is the senior pastor of Fellowship of Christians, a church he founded with some friends in the early 1970s during the Jesus movement. He leads worship and speaks regularly in various countries.

Louie Giglio and his wife, Shelley, head up the Passion movement in the U.S.A. and its music label, Six Steps Records. With a desire for the "name and renown" of the Lord (Isa. 26:8), they encourage thousands of college students in their pursuit of true worship.

Charlie Groves is married to Ali and they have three children. Since April 1999, he has been working as a worship pastor at Church of the Holy Spirit, a recent church plant in Cape Town, South Africa. Before that, he was a worship leader at Holy Trinity Brompton Anglican Church in London, England.

Charlie Hall is married to Kimberlyn, and with their two children, they live in Oklahoma City, Oklahoma. Ministering all over the United States with Passion, Charlie has written a number of songs including the well-known worship anthem "Salvation."

Tim Hughes is the writer of "Here I Am to Worship," as well as many other congregational songs. Based at Watford in England, he travels with Soul Survivor encouraging young people around the world to know Jesus and make Him known.

Chris Jack lives in Cambridge, England, and is chaplain and lecturer in applied theology at London Bible College. Specializing in the theology of worship, he regularly instructs students in the biblical foundations of our corporate worship.

Songwriter and hymnwriter **Graham Kendrick** has written over 500 worship compositions, including the widely sung "Shine Jesus Shine" and "The Servant King." A regular writer and speaker on the subject of worship-song content, he is married to Gill and lives in Surrey, England.

Based in Nashville, Tennessee, **Tom Lane** and his wife,
Patty, are part of Belmont Church. Ministering with
The Bridge, Tom longs to see creative young musicians
affirmed in their callings, while his own songs have
been distributed through Worship Together,
Integrity and Maranatha.

Martyn Layzell regularly leads worship at
Soul Survivor events and is an assistant pastor at
the Soul Survivor church in Watford, England. Married
to Emily, he is the writer of songs such as "Not By
Words" and "Sovereign Lord."

Based in Devon, England, **Andrew Maries**
works through the Keynote Trust to encourage
and stimulate music and worship in churches
at every level and in every style.

Robin Mark lives in Belfast, Ireland, with his wife,
Jacqueline, and their three children. He has led worship
in his local church, Christian Fellowship Church
in Belfast, for nine years. Robin is also a successful
businessman heading up his own company,
F. R. Mark and Associates.

Les Moir is head of Survivor Records in the United Kingdom and works closely with various youth organizations to resource the Church with fresh worship songs and sounds. He is also a bass player and former producer of worship albums by Graham Kendrick, Noel Richards and Matt Redman.

Sally Morganthaler is president of SJM Management Company, Inc., and functions as on-site worship consultant for Denver Seminar and Pathways Church. She has written books and articles and regularly teaches on worship in a postmodern culture.

Nigel Morris was born in the United Kingdom and moved to the United States in 1991 with his wife, Lynne, and their daughter, Sarah. He is on staff at Anaheim Vineyard, where he oversees both the worship-music department and the prison ministry.

Steve Nicholson is on the leadership board of the Vineyard movement in the United States and pastors a church in Evanston, Illinois. He is a strong encourager of many lead worshippers, and his leadership expertise brings wisdom and insight to the lives of many.

Based at Church of Christ the King, Brighton, **Paul Oakley** regularly leads worship at the 1,000-member church and with his band heads up the worship at many NFI youth events. His songs include "It's All About You (Jesus Lover of My Soul)" and "Because of You."

Graham Ord has been leading worship for nearly 20 years. He has recorded several CDs with Vineyard Music Group, as well as several solo projects. He is now based in Vancouver, British Columbia, where he works as a singer, songwriter and worship leader. He also speaks at conferences and training events on worship and songwriting.

Andy Park is worship overseer of the North Langley Vineyard church in Canada. Writer of "Only You" and numerous other Vineyard worship songs, he is also the author of *To Know You More: Cultivating the Heart of the Worship Leader.*

Andrew Philip, originally from South Africa, now lives in the United Kingdom. A producer, keyboard player and programer player for the likes of Soul Survivor and the Vineyard, he is also part of the *heartofworship.com* website team.

Andy Piercy is the music director at Holy Trinity Brompton Anglican Church in London, England. As a producer of albums by Rita Springer, Promise Keepers, Matt Redman and Cutting Edge (aka Delirious?), he has a great deal of experience overseeing the crafting and developing of congregational songs.

Mike Pilavachi leads Soul Survivor, a worship-centered youth movement that works with young people around the world. Having mentored many lead worshippers, authored the book *The Audience of One* and spoken regularly at various worship gatherings, Mike, without a doubt, has made worship his specialist subject.

Daphne Rademaker lives in Langley, Canada, with her husband, Darryl, where she leads worship at the Vineyard church. Daphne has also sung on many of the Vineyard Music releases.

Matt Redman is married to Beth and together they are part of Church of Christ the King in Brighton, England. Matt is the writer of the songs "Heart of Worship," "Let My Words Be Few" and "Befriended," as well as the author of *The Unquenchable Worshipper*. Matt is part of the team that edits the *heartofworship.com* website.

Noel Richards and his wife, Tricia, are based at Pioneer People Church in Surrey, England. He is the writer of songs such as "All Heaven Declares" and "To Be in Your Presence," and he coordinated the Champion of the World worship event at Wembley Stadium in 1997.

David Salmon is a musician, playwright, artist and graphic designer based at Soul Survivor in Watford, England. Through Littleboat Productions, David and his wife, Rosemary, pursue many ways to build bridges between worship and the arts. David also designed *The Heart of Worship Files* cover.

Kathryn Scott is married to Alan, and they live in Ireland, pastoring the Causeway Coast Vineyard. Kathryn leads worship on Vineyard Music Group's *Hungry* and *Surrender* CDs.

Rita Springer lives in Houston, Texas, and devotes much of her time and focus specifically on ministering to women. Involved with Vineyard Music Group, she has written numerous songs, as well as being involved globally in various conferences.

Texan **Chris Tomlin** regularly leads worship as part of the Passion team, alongside Louie Giglio. Chris is the writer of songs such as "We Fall Down" and "The Wonderful Cross." He and his band travel around the world leading the people of God in worship and teaching others to do the same.

Tommy Walker has led worship throughout the United States, Canada, Europe and Asia. Graduating in 1982 from Christ For The Nations Institute with a degree in practical theology, he gained a diploma in jazz and fusion at the Guitar Institute of Technology in Hollywood, California.

John David Walt, Jr., is vice president of community life and dean of the chapel at Asbury Theological Seminary in Kentucky. Cowriter of "The Wonderful Cross" with Chris Tomlin (and Isaac Watts!), he is also involved with the Passion movement of college students throughout the United States.

United Kingdom bass player **Matt Weeks** has been on worship teams with Brian Doerksen, Matt Redman, Brenton Brown, Tim Hughes and others. Because of his ability to play drums, trumpet, guitar and keyboards, Matt is in an ideal position to give insight into the many aspects of playing on a worship team.

Californian theologian **Don Williams** and his wife, Kathryn, live in San Diego, where Don has just retired as a Vineyard pastor. A former Hollywood pastor and professor of the New Testament at Fuller Theological Seminary, Don's activities now include working alongside Matt Redman in training young worship leaders in songwriting and theology.

John Willison is the worship pastor at the Evanston Vineyard church near Chicago, Illinois. Married to Carol, he is the writer of several Vineyard worship songs including "My Redeemer Lives" and "Jesus, I believe in You."

Based at Hillsong Church in Australia, **Darlene Zschech** is writer of "Shout to the Lord," one of the most universally sung worship songs in recent years. Married to Mark, she has recently written the book *Extravagant Worship* and also serves as executive director of Mercy Ministries Australia, a Christ-centered residential program for girls and women who suffer from eating disorders, drug addiction and emotional and/or physical abuse.